NUCLEAR FALLACY

NUCLEAR FALLACY
Dispelling the Myth of
Nuclear Strategy

MORTON H. HALPERIN

Ballinger Publishing Company
Cambridge, Massachusetts
A Subsidiary of Harper & Row, Publishers, Inc.

57466

U
263
H36
1987

#1583614

International Standard Book Number: 0-88730-114-2

Library of Congress Catalog Card Number: 86-32255

Printed in the United States of America

Library of Congress Cataloging-in-Publication Data

Halperin, Morton H.
  Nuclear fallacy.

  Bibliography: p.
  Includes index.
  1. Nuclear warfare. 2. Strategic forces—United States.
3. United States—Military policy. I. Title.
U263.H36 1987   355'.0217   86-32255
ISBN 0-88730-114-2

CONTENTS

ACKNOWLEDGMENTS

In returning to a field that I had left fifteen years ago, I imposed on many old friends and associates. It is therefore impossible for me to thank everyone who assisted in my efforts to become reacquainted with the literature and to produce what I hope will be a valuable contribution to the debate. At the risk of leaving someone out, I do want to thank those whose help and support were indispensable.

This project would not have begun but for the help and encouragement of David Ramage, then the president of the New World Foundation. A study group assembled jointly by the New World Foundation and the Center for Education on Nuclear War provided the first forum for the ideas that have found their way into this study.

Carol Franco, the publisher of Ballinger, expressed enthusiasm for this book long before there was a first outline. Her continued support and encouragement made it impossible to abandon the effort.

The decision by David Hamburg, president of the Carnegie Corporation, to involve that foundation in support of research on nuclear war provided resources to the three institutions that in turn supported the research and writing of the book. Fritz Mosher, the Carnegie project officer, was another source of critical support and encouragement throughout.

The research and thinking that ultimately produced this study were mostly done while I was in residence at the Kennedy School of Government at Harvard University. I am indebted to Dean Graham Allison and his colleagues in the Avoiding Nuclear War project for inviting me to Harvard and for providing pungent criticism of my early ideas. I benefited also from discussion at the seminars sponsored by the project.

The M.I.T. Center for International Studies provided support for the early phases of the writing of this study. I am indebted to George Rathjens and Jack Ruina for this support.

A number of people provided comments on a draft of the manuscript that was circulated at the end of 1985. I am indebted to Karen Mulhausser of the Center for Education on Nuclear War and Alton Frye of the Council on Foreign Relations for arranging seminars at which the manuscript was discussed.

Among the many people who provided detailed comments on some or all of that draft I am particularly indebted to McGeorge Bundy, Lynn Eden, Daniel Ellsberg, David Halperin, E. B. Harris, John Holdren, Frank von Hippel, Robert Levine, Madalene O'Donnell, James Rubin, and Leon Segal.

In the final phases of writing I was provided support from the No First Use Project of the Center for Education on Nuclear War created with support from the Carnegie Corporation. This made it possible for Madalene O'Donnell and William Fulton to work on the manuscript. Ms. O'Donnell tracked down all the sources for the study and prepared all the notes. She also incorporated many changes proposed by readers into the manuscript and in the process reworked the ideas. Most of all she pressed me to say what I really believed. Mr. Fulton edited much of the manuscript to make it accessible to a reader with no prior knowledge of the issues. He did so with unfailing sensitivity to the ideas being expressed and for the need to communicate them without diluting them.

Finally, I wish to express my appreciation to the MacArthur Foundation, which awarded one of its fellowships to me. This extraordinary grant relieved me of the burden of financial concerns and made it possible for me to devote my own time to the completion of this manuscript. While numerous events conspired to delay its completion, it is no exaggeration to say it might well not have been completed at all but for the generosity of the MacArthur Foundation.

Both before and after I wrote this book I was affiliated with the American Civil Liberties Union and with the Center for National Security Studies. However, neither the ACLU nor the Center was associated in any way with this undertaking. The views expressed are entirely my own.

While being grateful for all of this assistance and more, I remain responsible for the content of this book.

Morton H. Halperin

Washington, D.C.
1 December 1986

INTRODUCTION

The military forces of the United States are equipped, trained, and deployed based on the assumption that nuclear explosive devices can and should be used to fight and win wars. Nuclear devices are carried with naval vessels at sea; with American air and ground forces at their bases in Europe, Korea, and perhaps elsewhere; and with U.S. forces waiting to be sent abroad.

In fact, at any instant, 5,000 of the 25,000 nuclear devices in the American arsenal are ready to be fired within minutes at any potential adversary anywhere in the world. These "alert" forces include one-third of the warheads carried on bombers, half of the submarines carrying long-range missiles, nearly all of the intercontinental ballistic missiles (ICBMs) based in the United States, as well as some warheads stationed abroad. The destructive capacity of only those warheads on alert is such that any country designated for attack could be totally destroyed within minutes. Many believe that the short- and long-term effects of such an attack may destroy not only that nation but all of human civilization.

This nuclear posture is not simply a charade staged to scare others but never used. Nor does it exist simply for responding to the use of nuclear devices by others. This deployment reflects American military policy, which calls for the initiation of the use of nuclear "weapons" whenever "necessary."

Proposals to reduce the risk of nuclear war generally focus on particular weapons systems as they are built and deployed or on new warheads as they are tested. But in my view, these are specific symptoms, not the abiding causes, of the problem. The deeper questions that must be debated by the American public are ones that elected officials rarely, if ever, discuss. What, precisely, does the United States rely on nuclear weapons to do? And what *should* it rely on them to do?

For a short time during the 1940s, the United States had a monopoly on nuclear weapons and attempted to use it to deter Soviet aggression in Europe. American forces stood prepared to launch a nuclear attack against the Soviet Union in response to nonnuclear Soviet aggression or anticipated aggression.

Ever since, and despite the loss of that monopoly, the role of American nuclear weapons has remained virtually unchanged. Nuclear weapons and nuclear threats have been wielded to deter the Soviet Union from firing its nuclear weapons, to deter the Soviets from using their conventional forces, and to deter other potential adversaries from taking actions that conflict with American interests. At the same time, the U.S. military has been led to believe that nuclear weapons can compensate for shortcomings in conventional forces.

The strategic nuclear balance between the United States and the Soviet Union has changed tremendously since the underpinnings of American nuclear policy were established forty years ago. Today the two countries have some 20,000 nuclear warheads aimed at each other. And American forces continue preparations to launch a nuclear attack against the Soviet Union—even before the Soviets have used nuclear weapons. The United States has built a doomsday machine that reaches around the globe and threatens to escape control.

This doomsday machine is built upon the assumption that nuclear warheads are, in fact, *weapons* that can be used to fight and win wars. I believe this assumption must be challenged. Nuclear explosive devices, as I prefer to call them, might possibly serve as demonstrations of military will and determination, as they did in Hiroshima and Nagasaki. But they are not weapons because they cannot be used to any real advantage on a battlefield without destroying what they are intended to defend. No one knows how to win a nuclear war. Yet nuclear devices are integrated into all aspects of U.S. military strategy worldwide.

This American nuclear posture increases the risk of nuclear war in a number of ways. First, inherent in this posture is the assumption that it is important to use nuclear weapons quickly, enormously compressing decision-making time and increasing the pressure on U.S. leaders to use nuclear devices in response to attack, whether real or imagined. Second, the integration of nuclear weapons with conventional forces increases the risk that the United States would be forced to choose between using nuclear weapons quickly or allowing them (or the military units possessing them) to be captured—the use-them-or-lose-them phenomenon. Third, the existing posture increases the risk of accidental or unauthorized war. In a crisis the controls over nuclear forces are loosened, increasing the chances of an accidental firing of nuclear weapons.

Fourth, America's public commitment to using nuclear weapons in a wide range of circumstances may become a self-fulfilling prophesy. When confronted with a serious threat, the United States might have little choice but to react by unleashing a nuclear war. In pursuing the "nuclear option," the United States may have precluded other options. Fifth, American nuclear policy creates strong domestic resistance to potentially beneficial arms control proposals that seek to reduce reliance on nuclear weapons. Finally, in any serious crisis, Soviet military planners and leaders, well aware that the United States might use nuclear weapons first, would be prepared to launch a preemptive nuclear attack of their own.

Most Americans are unaware of even the basic outlines of U.S. nuclear policy. Many misguidedly believe that the United States would never initiate the use of nuclear weapons under any circumstances. Many others assume that no measure short of comprehensive disarmament or a fundamental change in the nature of Soviet-American relations would effectively diminish the possibility of nuclear war. Thus, those who fear that nuclear war may occur see possibilities for progress only in nuclear disarmament, more general disarmament, détente, or world government.

There is, however, nothing immutable about current American nuclear policy. It developed out of conscious presidential policy choices and the reaction of the military services to those choices. Americans can change U.S. nuclear policy if they decide to do so.

The simple truth, as I will demonstrate in this book, is that American policy can be changed to reduce significantly the likelihood of nuclear war. These changes can be made without waiting for international agreements or improvements in the state of Soviet-American political relations. If implemented correctly, they will increase America's ability to achieve its diplomatic and military objectives by safer and more effective means.

Considerable political will must motivate such a policy change. But before we can hope to generate that political will, the American people must come to understand that policies can be changed and that important choices are there to be made. I hope this book will help bring these choices to light.

1 A BRIEF HISTORY OF AMERICAN NUCLEAR POLICY

The Manhattan Project, the all-out top-secret effort to make the first atomic bomb during World War II, was initially justified by the belief that the Germans had a substantial program to develop atomic weapons, and, therefore, the Allies might need their own atomic weapons to win the war. By the end of 1944, the United States knew Germany was not working on the atom bomb; nonetheless, the Manhattan Project, clearly on the road to success, was completed and the United States dropped two atomic bombs on Japan.[1]

In many ways, the decision-making process that led to the bombing of Hiroshima and Nagasaki serves as a metaphor for the development of nuclear policy in the United States. It was not set in place in a single, inevitable act. Rather, it arose from decisions made by President Truman after consultation with the military services.

Similarly, American nuclear policy as it developed under Truman, Eisenhower, and Kennedy was not an inevitability. It too arose from presidential directives and actions taken by the military services in both influencing those directives and carrying them out. Over time, it became increasingly difficult to alter the direction of American nuclear policy, so that

President Kennedy attained only limited success in his attempts to unravel Eisenhower-era policies. (Since then, nuclear policies have remained virtually unchanged.) This chapter traces these policies as they have been reflected in doctrine, weapons, and deployment and examines the interaction between presidential directives and service actions.

HIROSHIMA REVISITED

For more than forty years, debate has continued over why President Truman decided, in August of 1945, to drop the world's first atomic bomb on Hiroshima. Truman himself often justified his action, in later years, by citing the U.S. military estimate that defeating Japan by conventional means would have resulted in as many as 1 million additional American casualties. Revisionist accounts have argued that Truman dropped the bomb not to win the war (Japan was close to surrender at the time) but to scare the Russians.

From what we know of Truman's decision, we can be confident of three things. First, Truman received a military assessment that conventional military action would lead to 1 million or more American casualties. Second, he believed that estimate and acted upon it. And third, the assessment was false. It was determined not by the facts but, primarily, by the structure of American military forces—a structure that has played a major role in U.S. nuclear policy over the years.

Most Americans assumed during World War II, and still believe, that the four branches of the military service (army, navy, marines, and air force, then a part of the army known as the army air forces) were following an integrated military plan to defeat the Japanese and were working together under the command of General Douglas MacArthur to end the war as quickly as possible. But the reality was quite different.

In 1945 there was little integration of military advice and operations. The Joint Chiefs of Staff and the Secretary of Defense, with their staffs independent of individual military branches, did not exist. In fact, each service was fighting its own war. Each was determined to defeat the Japanese by using only those forces under its control, believing that its own forces would be sufficient. And in reaching separate judgments about how long the war would take, each service calculated only the consequences of its own military power.

The army focused on the invasion and conquest of Japan. Army doctrine held that an enemy could be defeated only by the physical conquest of its territory and the defeat of its ground forces. From the army's perspective, this doctrine was borne out by the surrender of Germany, which came only after its armies had been defeated and Allied forces occupied much of the territory of the Third Reich. The impact of naval operations and of the massive strategic bombing by the air force were, in the army's view, negligible.

For the navy and the marine corps, which were limited to a subordinate role in the European war, the battle in the Pacific was seen as an opportunity to demonstrate the utility of war at sea, naval blockades, and amphibious assault operations by the marines. Unlike their counterparts in the army, navy and marine leaders did not believe that the invasion of Japan would be necessary. They thought that because Japan was an island nation, naval operations would force its surrender before the army would be ready to mount an all-out assault.

The air force held a similarly narrow view. Air force leaders were determined to create a separate service, but to do so they had to prove that air power was capable of winning a war on its own, not merely of providing close support for ground combat operations. The doctrine they proposed was "strategic bombing," which holds that it is possible to defeat the enemy by bombing his war-production facilities and cities, thus destroying his capacity to wage war and the will of his people to fight. (Strategic bombing has remained a key element of American nuclear policy throughout the postwar era.)

But initial studies in Europe, which indicated that the value of the massive strategic bombing against Hitler had been greatly exaggerated, jeopardized the air force's effort to gain autonomy. Air force leaders argued that neither an invasion of Japan nor a blockade would be necessary because strategic bombing could force a Japanese surrender.

When asked to render a unified judgment of how long it would take to defeat Japan and with what number of casualties, the services negotiated an estimate to which each could subscribe. But no one sought to calculate the cumulative effect of the activities of all of the military services. Moreover, the military's calculations considered only military force; none of the services took account of the possibilities of diplomacy. They assumed that Japan would surrender only when it was physically unable to wage war any longer.

In fact, we now know that at this time some Japanese military and political leaders were desperately seeking to arrange a surrender.[2] The entire leadership knew there was no hope of victory. While some military officers were determined to fight on to the death, others in the military, and some civilian leaders, were eager to engineer an end to the war. They wanted to curtail the useless suffering of the Japanese people and also prevent the Russians from seizing Japanese territory. All were united in the belief that their primary goal in surrender was to preserve the life of the emperor and his symbolic status as the leader of the Japanese nation. No Japanese leader would contemplate surrender without that assurance.

Thus, as President Truman considered what course to take, he was unaware of two important facts: that the Japanese were near surrender and that the joint military estimate of American casualties was unrealistically high. Furthermore, he was under tremendous pressure from the American public to end the war as quickly as possible.

Throughout 1945, Truman searched for an effective use for the atomic bomb. Significantly, neither Truman himself nor his key advisers seriously considered transferring the weapon to the military. Had Truman viewed the atomic bomb as just another military weapon, he would have turned it over to MacArthur, who, in all likelihood, would have integrated its use into plans for invading the main Japanese islands. Nor did Truman or his advisers seriously consider not using the bombs at all.

Truman eventually settled on what seemed, to him, a middle course—the limited use of atomic bombs as a "terrorist" device against two Japanese cities. To this day, it is unclear whether the bombings considerably shortened the war. Japan did surrender following the bombings—but only after its leaders were confident that the Allied powers would respect the emperor, both as a person and in his ceremonial role. However, we do know that use of the atomic bomb was not *necessary* to end the war or even to end it without an invasion.

Truman's experience with nuclear diplomacy foreshadowed that of his successors in three respects. First, the critical variables in ending the war were diplomatic negotiations and the overwhelming superiority of American conventional military forces—not the power of "The Bomb." Second, when faced with a decision actually to use nuclear weapons, Truman was extremely reluctant to consider them for tactical military purposes on the battlefield; instead, he deployed them solely for the strategic goal of speeding surrender. And third, the military advice he received was largely skewed by the internal decision-making structure of the military and the competing interests of each service.

POSTWAR POLICY

After the war, Truman was confronted with two major decisions regarding nuclear policy. First, assuming that the United States would proceed with the research and manufacture of nuclear warheads, what agency would perform these tasks? And second, what role would the threat of the use of these devices play in U.S. security policy?

The military's answers to these questions were simple. Nuclear devices were weapons, and, as such, their manufacture should be the responsibility of the military services. In the military's view, nuclear weapons should be available for use in all militarily appropriate situations. In fact, the Joint Chiefs' plans for using nuclear weapons, presented in a 1947 memorandum, assumed their unrestricted use.[3]

But Truman was not so sure. Despite the apparent ease with which he had come to the decision to drop the atomic bombs on Hiroshima and Nagasaki, Truman recognized that there was something very different about nuclear devices. As he once explained: "You have got to understand that this isn't a military weapon. It is used to wipe out women, children, and unarmed people, and not for military use. So we have to treat this differently from rifles and cannon and ordinary things like that."[4]

Truman supported the creation of an extraordinary institution called the Atomic Energy Commission (AEC), which was established by the Atomic Energy Act of 1946. The AEC had responsibility not only for manufacturing nuclear weapons, as does its contemporary successor, the Department of Energy, but also for maintaining the nuclear arsenal. The weapons were held by the AEC, to be turned over to the military only upon presidential authorization.

The law also made it clear that atomic weapons could be used only with the explicit authority of the president. Truman refused to delegate this authority or to indicate in advance whether he would authorize the use of nuclear bombs in a crisis or war. He did allow the military to draw up plans for the use of nuclear weapons but stated his resolve to control that use directly. In future nuclear encounters, he apparently intended to select a very limited number of targets and to "terrorize" his enemies rather than win a specific battle. (NSC-30, the official atomic policy directive, recognized the need for the military to plan for using atomic weapons but gave the decision of when and how to use the bombs to the president.) However, Truman did not direct the military to plan for the terrorist option, and the Joint Chiefs did not do so. Instead, early military plans called for massive air strikes against Soviet targets.[5]

The military services fought hard against the decision not to turn over the finished atomic bombs to them. They argued that they needed the warheads for training purposes and that the weapons should reside with the forces that would use them. Time and again, they petitioned Truman, but repeatedly, with the energetic support of David Lilienthal, chairman of the AEC, the president resisted.[6]

The consensus among Truman's national security advisers was not to push the president for a decision to pre-delegate the authority to use nuclear weapons or even to specify the circumstances under which they would be used.[7] They recognized that any decision was likely to leak out and create problems with the public and with America's allies. Then, as now, American and allied public opinion was divided. Some people desperately wanted guarantees that nuclear weapons would be used in certain situations. Others opposed the use of nuclear weapons under any circumstances. Moreover, explicit U.S. reliance on nuclear threats to deter conventional attack would directly contradict public efforts to abolish nuclear weapons by international agreement.[8]

Still, Truman and his advisers believed the nuclear arsenal was essential to detering Soviet conventional aggression, particularly in Europe. Following the virtual dismantling of the American military forces after the war, the conventional forces that would be needed to defeat a Soviet move westward into Europe simply were not in place. For this reason, a "no first use" policy was not considered possible.

Nonetheless, Truman resisted using nuclear weapons in Korea and refused to define the circumstances under which he actually might authorize their use. Given this reticence and the scarcity of finished weapons at the time, military leaders grew skeptical that atomic warheads would be available for combat.

Truman's belief that American nuclear power was necessary to deter Soviet aggression led naturally to a concern about what would happen when the Kremlin had the bomb as well. Beginning in 1949, he authorized a vast increase in the capacity to produce nuclear material. And upon learning that the Soviet atomic program was progressing much more quickly than the intelligence community had predicted, he authorized the development of the "super," or hydrogen, bomb.

Although Truman authorized efforts through the United Nations to negotiate the total elimination of nuclear devices, he never reconciled this aim with his belief that the threat of first use of nuclear bombs was necessary to deter Soviet aggression in Europe and throughout the world. Most of Truman's advisers, unsure of his position, were willing to duck the argument. And when his proposals for international control of nuclear devices stalled in 1947, Truman himself largely abandoned the effort and accepted the growing role of nuclear weapons in American defense policy.[9]

However, two lonely and prophetic statesmen, one in the U.S. Senate and one inside the bureaucracy, were beginning to question the consequences of the first-use policy that had been adopted with little internal discussion and even less public debate.

In 1949, Senator Ralph Flanders, a Republican from Vermont, introduced a resolution stating that "the atomic bomb, like biological warfare and wholesale poisoning, is not properly a military device directed against the armed forces of the enemy, but is rather a means for the mass murder of civilians."[10] Flanders called on the United States to adopt a public policy that it would not use nuclear devices except in retaliation for their use by others—in short, a no-first-use policy. But there was little public response.[11]

A similar proposal was made within the administration by George Kennan, head of the State Department Policy Planning Staff. His suggestion to adopt a no-first-use policy also went without support, and his efforts to stimulate an internal debate were equally fruitless. Kennan wrote a memorandum in the fall of 1949 that he considered "one of the most important, if not the most important, of all the documents I ever wrote in government."[12] In the memorandum he argued that the United States had a fundamental choice to make regarding nuclear weapons. The United States could regard nuclear weapons either as "something which we have resolved, in the face of all the moral and other factors concerned, to employ forthwith and unhesitatingly at the outset of any great military conflict" or as "something superfluous to our basic military posture—as something that we are compelled to hold against the possibility that they might be used by our opponents."[13]

The course of American nuclear policy hinged on how that question was answered, Kennan said. He advocated choosing the second alternative, which would mean that the United

States should "take care not to build up a reliance upon them in our military planning." However, his plea for recognizing this fundamental distinction between the two policies was not heeded in the remaining years of the Truman administration.

Though President Eisenhower was to provide what appeared to be clear, if ill-conceived, answers early in his term in office, this same question remains at the heart of nuclear policy debates in the United States.

THE EISENHOWER LEGACY

If Harry Truman bears responsibility for the doctrine that nuclear devices can be used to actively promote the interests of the United States, rather than simply preventing their use by others, Dwight Eisenhower bears responsibility for the current nuclear structure, which treats nuclear devices as weapons. Soon after his inauguration as president in 1954, Eisenhower initiated two measures that swept away the limits Truman had established on the treatment of nuclear devices. These two steps led inexorably to the current worldwide nuclear deployments.

In the first of these directives the AEC was ordered gradually to transfer custody of its stockpile of nuclear devices and nonnuclear components to the military. The military, in turn, was authorized to disperse these devices to U.S. forces throughout the world. This decision to reduce civilian control has never been seriously reconsidered by American policymakers and remains in force today.

The second measure took the form of a presidential directive, NSC 162/1. It consisted of a single sentence buried in a general National Security Council document, known as the Basic National Security Policy, approved by Eisenhower on October 30, 1953. The ominous sentence reads: "In the event of hostilities, the United States will consider nuclear weapons to be as available for use as other munitions."[14]

As we will see, Eisenhower's subsequent reactions to proposals for the bureaucracy to actually use nuclear weapons in various crises suggest that he may not have meant to set in motion quite so sweeping a change in deployments and war plans. Be that as it may, the statement was official policy, and it profoundly altered every aspect of U.S. national security policy, particularly during the first half of the Eisenhower administration.

These two directives drastically increased the danger of nuclear war by changing the American military establishment from a collection of conventional fighting units into a military body that equips and trains itself on the assumption that nuclear devices will be used in combat. Prior to the issuance of these directives, the military services were ambivalent about the proper role of nuclear weapons. On the one hand, the devices had enormous explosive power and, if used, would revolutionize warfare among nations. Furthermore, Truman, despite his hesitancy to use them, had authorized their production in large numbers. On the other hand, the military was reluctant to rely on weapons controlled by civilians (the president and the AEC), who would clearly be loath to contemplate their use in a crisis.

But the Eisenhower directives effectively removed these uncertainties. They permitted—indeed forced—the military to integrate nuclear weapons into all aspects of force procurement, deployment, and war planning. For the next five years, the military carried out these directives to their logical conclusions, which had staggering implications. To understand these implications fully, we must examine the directives' impact on various aspects of national security.

Procurement

The military services must continually make decisions about future military requirements for weapons systems such as airplanes, missiles, and tanks. Prior to the Eisenhower directive, these systems were developed primarily for the delivery of conventional bombs. Once NSC 162/1 was approved, however, all delivery systems began to be designed on the assumption that they would be used only for the delivery of nuclear weapons.

Indeed, during this period, nuclear devices were referred to in internal Pentagon memoranda and war plans as "conventional" weapons, and nonnuclear weapons were called obsolete "iron bombs."[15] The sweeping nature of NSC 162/1 left no room for any military service to retain the ability or option of conducting large-scale nonnuclear operations. Rather, each service began to equip all of its forces with nuclear weapons and to develop nuclear weapons for every contingency. Nonnuclear forces were considered obsolete.

The air force removed all racks for conventional bombs from its bombers, entirely denying itself a conventional bombing capability.[16] The navy equipped its ships and designed its planes for delivery of nuclear weapons. The army developed small artillery pieces to deliver nuclear weapons. Forces on alert were equipped with nuclear devices. From 1953 to 1958, the military, acting on Eisenhower's directives, set in motion the tremendous "nuclearization" of American and allied forces that still exists.

The result was that the American capacity to fight conventionally was substantially and deliberately reduced. In future crises, the military would cite the shortcomings in its ability to wage conventional war as evidence that if the United States planned to fight, the president would have to permit the use of nuclear weapons. Fortunately, as we will see, Eisenhower and his successors showed considerable caution in evaluating such advice during crisis situations.

Some of the military's procurement policies *were* partially reversed in the late 1950s. After observing Eisenhower's clear reluctance to use nuclear weapons in Korea and Quemoy, which I will discuss in the next chapter, military leaders began hedging their bets and reestablishing conventional capabilities. Even though they pulled back from sole dependence on nuclear defense, however, they retained most of the essential characteristics of the nuclear posture.

Dispersion

The second and more politically sensitive step in implementing NSC 162/1 was to disperse the nuclear weapons with

American forces stationed overseas. NSC 162/1 authorized and set the procedure for deployment of nuclear weapons on the territory of other sovereign states. The entire discussion of the issue reads as follows:

> (1) . . . Where the consent of an ally is required for the use of these weapons from U.S. bases on the territory of such ally, the United States should promptly obtain the advance consent of such ally for such use. The United States should also seek, as and when feasible, the understanding and approval of this policy by free nations.
>
> (2) This policy should not be made public without further consideration by the National Security Council.[17]

Thus, without public debate or even public knowledge, the U.S. government determined not only to use nuclear devices in any future conflict but also to disperse them throughout the world. At the same time, the State Department and the military services sought support from American allies for the policy of using nuclear devices on the battlefield and, more concretely, sought permission to fire nuclear weapons from their territory.

The secrecy surrounding American nuclear policy in the 1950s was not an attempt to keep information from the Soviet Union. In fact, American leaders *wanted* the Kremlin to believe that the United States would use nuclear devices quickly in the event of hostilities. Rather, the secrecy arose from American leaders' fears that making the directive public would provoke intense opposition at home and particularly in Europe, where the policy was to be implemented first.

American efforts to deploy nuclear devices on allied territory without public acknowledgment were veiled in a euphemistic phrase pointing out the need to "educate American allies on the realities of the atomic age." In private, this phrase meant that the allies were told that they must permit nuclear weapons to be stored on their territory; that they must give blanket permission for the United States to fire those weapons; that they should support a U.S. decision to use nuclear weapons in any military conflict; and that they should not explain or defend this policy publicly. In Europe, where this new policy was applied first, American allies were threatened with the withdrawal of all U.S. military forces if they did not consent to the plan.

This forced choice created a dilemma for all European nations. An American military presence was extremely important to European leaders, yet antinuclear feeling among the European people was intense, and remains so today. The problem was especially acute for the German government, which had renounced its own nuclear capability and was now being told that its armies would be able to fight only with weapons provided by another nation. For the British and French, the choice spurred the continued development of their own nuclear devices to mitigate their reliance on American nuclear forces.

Some nations, such as Denmark and Norway (and, outside of Europe, Japan), prohibited the storage of nuclear weapons on their territory because of strong public opposition. So far as is known, the American military accommodated itself to these demands.

Given Eisenhower's great stature as a war hero and the early stage of the arms race, Eisenhower truly had an opportunity to determine the course of the nuclear age at the beginning of his administration. Had he adopted Kennan's no-first-use proposal, the world today might be very different. "Educating our allies to the realities of the atomic age" would have meant educating them to the fact that nuclear devices were not, in fact, weapons, and could be deployed only to prevent their use by the Soviet Union or other nations. The United States would have developed and maintained a nuclear arsenal on its own territory sufficient to deter the use of nuclear weapons by the Soviet Union against American allies, leaving open the possibility of deploying a small number of weapons to Europe in a crisis to strengthen the threat of retaliation.

The American message to Europeans and other allies would have been that the West must depend on conventional weapons and diplomacy for its security, as all nations had in the past. Given the general deference to American views and the strong antinuclear sentiment in their own countries, it is doubtful that any U.S. allies would have challenged this decision.[18] Rather than viewing antinuclear movements and proposals for disarmament as threats to American interests, the United States could have embraced them and forged a common cause with them in the effort to prevent other nations from acquiring nuclear weapons.

Instead, nuclear devices were stored on the soil of every allied country that would accept them, and future efforts to modify or rescind Eisenhower's nuclear directive became increasingly difficult.

War Plans and Training Programs

With the worldwide deployment of nuclear weapons, military analysts sought to develop effective plans for fighting on the "atomic battlefield."[19] They assumed that atomic weapons would complement more traditional forces. The army, for example, began planning so-called pentomic divisions—divisions especially designed to engage in nuclear combat.[20] The 1961 Pacific Air Force command training manual included this directive:

> Nuclear training will in every instance take precedence over non-nuclear familiarization and qualification. It is emphasized that conventional training will not be accomplished at the expense of the higher priority nuclear training required by this manual. Non-MSF units will restrict conventional familiarization to the accomplishment of only one event per aircrew per year.[21]

This strategic dependence on nuclear weaponry and the intention to initiate the use of nuclear devices if it was deemed advisable were presented to the public in general terms. The most specific statement came in Secretary of State John Foster Dulles's famous "massive retaliation" speech, delivered in 1954 to the Council of Foreign Relations.

Dulles announced that the United States would henceforth "depend primarily upon a great capacity to retaliate instantly, by means and at places of our own choosing."[22] The clear implication was that the United States would respond even to local aggression with nuclear retaliation. The strategy was immediately criticized by civilian and military analysts as dangerous and incredible. To rely on nuclear weapons in all contingencies, they argued, would unnecessarily invite Soviet retaliation and leave the United States without the ability to respond proportionately to limited aggression. Moreover, there was the danger that Soviet leaders might interpret the policy as a bluff and respond by testing U.S. resolve.

By the late 1950s, the reaction to the Dulles speech, along with Eisenhower's refusal to authorize in advance the use of nuclear weapons in particular crises, among other factors led to a modification in how the services treated nuclear weapons. Also critical to producing these changes was an increasingly vocal core of military leaders skeptical of reliance on nuclear weapons, though often for very different reasons. Some, such as General Matthew B. Ridgway, questioned the military effectiveness of nuclear weapons in a tactical battlefield situation.[23] Others simply doubted that any president would make nuclear weapons available to the military in a war or crisis. Still others, such as General Maxwell D. Taylor, were concerned that American conventional forces would be neglected or unnecessarily burdened by nuclear forces.[24]

In short, by the end of Eisenhower's presidency, the language in NSC 162/1 remained unchanged, but the military had reestablished some capability to fight with conventional forces and rhetoric about massive retaliation had been toned down. It remained for the Kennedy administration to reconsider the policy and to make some formal changes.

THE KENNEDY REEVALUATION

President John F. Kennedy and his advisers were extremely skeptical of the heavy reliance placed on nuclear devices by the Eisenhower administration. In particular, they were doubtful that so-called battlefield, or tactical, nuclear weapons could be used effectively without prompting escalation to general war. They sought instead to develop a capability for sustained conventional combat operations in Europe, as well as elsewhere in the world, so that it would be unnecessary to initiate the use of nuclear weapons. Thus, with regard to short-range and theater nuclear weapons deployed abroad, the Kennedy administration tried to revise the policies of past presidents. However, in the planning of strategic forces, Kennedy treated nuclear devices more like other, conventional weapons.

Soon after becoming president, Kennedy indicated that the original Eisenhower directive no longer held, and he ordered the military to concentrate on training for conventional war. Gaining approval of alternate language describing if and when nuclear weapons would be used, however, proved to be more difficult. Some members of the new administration advocated a no-first-use position, but they were in the minority. The dominant opinion was that the United States needed to leave open the option of initiating the use of nuclear weapons. To persuade NATO countries to build up their conventional forces and reduce reliance on nuclear weapons, the Kennedy administration had to reassure them that the United States remained willing to escalate to nuclear weapons first, if necessary, to prevent defeat in Europe.

Having been told for some eight years that nuclear weapons were essential to the defense of Europe, however, NATO leaders were not ready suddenly to believe the opposite nor to pay the political cost of reversing direction. Indeed, it was not until 1968 that NATO formally instituted the policy of "flexible response," which called for a delay in the use of nuclear weapons.

Taken at face value, the change in policy from massive retaliation to flexible response was significant. Rather than treating nuclear devices as regular weapons available in any conflict, a flexible response strategy viewed them as special weapons to be used only when necessary to prevent defeat. However, it had a relatively limited effect on U.S. nuclear deployments and planning around the world.

Development and procurement policy during the Eisenhower administration had, without formal change, drifted toward flexible response once the military recognized Eisenhower's reluctance to authorize first use of nuclear devices.

The Kennedy administration did not push implementation of its policy far enough to decisively influence procurement, deployment, or war planning. The services were already committed to developing the capacity to fight a nuclear war. Military planners believed that American conventional forces alone were not capable of defeating a Sino-Soviet military threat. Nuclear systems were already dispersed around the world, and systems designed primarily, if not exclusively, for the delivery of nuclear weapons were in the field.

Having made this investment, the military services were unwilling to accept a new doctrine. The army did abandon plans for the nuclear pentomic divisions and the air force replaced the racks for conventional bombs, but few other changes were made in military capability.

Moreover, from the military perspective there was no fundamental change in strategy. Though the intent of flexible response was to ensure that any use of nuclear weapons would be late and limited, the language of the new doctrine permitted the use of nuclear devices when "necessary." Because most military officers believed there was an irreversible imbalance in conventional forces, they assumed that even under the new policy any major war would soon turn into a nuclear war, and that was what they should prepare for.

Thus, despite the Kennedy administration's skepticism about the utility of nuclear devices, it was unable, for a variety of bureaucratic, political, and diplomatic reasons, to halt the dispersal of nuclear devices throughout the world. U.S. government officials continued to "educate" American allies about the need to permit the weapons to be stored on their territory. In fact, most of the 7,000 nuclear weapons that the Eisenhower administration had earmarked for NATO countries were not actually deployed until the early 1960s, when Kennedy was president. Ironically, the Kennedy administration came under attack in some quarters for attempting to denuclearize Europe at precisely the time the United States was shipping vast quantities of nuclear devices to NATO countries. It was for this reason that in 1967 Secre-

tary of Defense Robert McNamara for the first time officially revealed that the United States stored nuclear weapons in Europe.

The Kennedy administration lost an opportunity to adopt
a no-first-use policy as well. The only time in the nuclear age
that a significant number of no-first-use advocates occupied
high positions within the government was during the early
1960s.[25] But, again, several factors converged to prevent
adopting no first use. Among them was the strong opposition
from European leaders who were concerned about Soviet
intentions in Western Europe. Skeptics in the United States
confused a *revised* American commitment to Europe with a
reduced American commitment, and some military officers
and their allies in Congress reinforced this mistaken view.
Though Kennedy and his advisers were committed to a reduced reliance on nuclear weapons, they were not sufficiently convinced of the value of a no-first-use policy to take on
the various constituencies opposed to it.

The most influential factor at that time—and the one that
has changed most drastically since the early 1960s—was public opinion.[26] Twenty-five years ago, public opinion in the
United States was not heavily weighted against current
American nuclear policy, as it is today. The political left was
preoccupied with efforts to promote general disarmament;
nuclear devices were not separated from conventional military power in their view. And the "arms control community"
that has grown up since then—academicians, public interest
groups, and others who accept America's need for armed defense but question its reliance on nuclear weapons—simply
did not exist. Almost the only public opinion source of pressure on the Kennedy administration was the right—those
who objected to any move away from nuclear weapons.

The nature of the press leaks from inside the Kennedy
administration was a good indicator of the political mood of
the times. Leaks reveal not only who is losing in an internal
policy battle but also who believes they have the support of
the public. Administration insiders will go public only if they
are convinced that the public and Congress are on their side.

The Kennedy administration was plagued with leaks about its alleged efforts to denuclearize Europe and to adopt a no-first-use policy. The leaks prompted hearty denunciations of these efforts from members of Congress, the press, and much of the attentive public. In response, administration officials were forced to reiterate their determination to use nuclear weapons whenever "necessary." These statements signaled the national security bureaucracy that, despite the Kennedy administration's earlier efforts, little had really changed.

STRATEGIC WEAPONS

In the area of strategic nuclear forces, the Kennedy administration moved decisively toward viewing nuclear devices as weapons and possible instruments of policy.

The Eisenhower administration had shown little interest in military planning for the use of strategic nuclear weapons against targets in the Soviet Union. Most of the strategic nuclear bombs in existence during the 1950s were located in Air Force Strategic Air Command bombers; thus, their use was subject to the air force doctrine of strategic bombing. This meant that the force was designed and programmed to launch a massive strike against the full range of targets in the Soviet bloc, including military forces and industrial capability, as soon as war began. The theory was that this decisive blow would quickly bring whatever ground war was in progress to a halt with a Soviet surrender. There was some logic to the strategy—at least as a threat—so long as the Soviets had no capacity to respond with their own long-range nuclear forces against the United States.

When President Kennedy took office, it was clear that the situation on which this strategy was based would soon change. The Soviet Union was rapidly developing the capacity to destroy the United States in retaliation for an American nuclear attack on the Soviet homeland. One U.S. response could have been—and, I will argue, should have been—to remove a first strategic strike from authorized policy. This the Kennedy team was not willing to do. Though skeptical of the utility of battlefield nuclear weapons, many of the administration's members believed that the United States had to be able to threaten credibly the first use of American strategic forces.

Because the United States would not admit publicly that it might drop nuclear weapons on the Soviet Union before the Soviets attacked the United States, arguments about strategic nuclear options were debated as if the question was how to respond to a Soviet nuclear attack. Inside the government, however, it was understood that the key issue was what the United States would do if it *initiated* the strategic exchange in response to a Soviet conventional attack in Europe or elsewhere.

The strategy Kennedy's advisers devised was known variously as "no-cities," "war-fighting," and "damage limitation." As McNamara put it in one speech, "Basic military strategy in a possible general nuclear war should be approached in much the same way that more conventional military operations have been regarded in the past."[27] In other words, the United States should target military forces, not civilian installations, and negotiate an end to the conflict before either nation is destroyed.

The Kennedy administration directed the military to develop a range of options that it hoped would permit limited and controlled nuclear strikes, thereby making credible the threat to attack the Soviet Union with nuclear devices in response to a Soviet conventional attack anywhere in the world. These directives also provided the rationale for developing strategic nuclear forces capable of destroying Soviet strategic nuclear forces, including Soviet missiles deployed in hardened missile silos.

It was certainly ironic, then, that the Kennedy administration came under fire for adopting the policy of "assured destruction." Assured destruction, or what its critics called MAD (mutual assured destruction), is widely perceived as an American policy under which continued peace relies on the assurance that both the United States and the Soviet Union would be destroyed in a nuclear war. It is true that soon after announcing the "no-cities" doctrine, Secretary of Defense

McNamara stated that the United States would develop strategic nuclear forces sufficient to absorb a Soviet first strike and then to destroy a substantial portion of Soviet cities and industries. Although critics took this to mean that the United States would respond to a Soviet attack by seeking to destroy Soviet cities, such a response was never the intent, and this view was never embodied in U.S. nuclear war plans.

Assured destruction was simply intended as a criterion for determining how large American strategic forces should be. It was consistent with the targeting of general industrial capability (and therefore, of cities) as well as of military targets. McNamara, in "quantifying" general destruction, used it as a management device to justify turning down requests for increases in strategic forces. The doctrine was *not* used to prohibit the development of strategic forces capable of attacking Soviet military targets; the United States already had that capability and would continue to develop and expand it. Nor was assured destruction ever the basis for developing war plans; the United States continued to maintain the option of attacking and destroying Soviet strategic forces before they were fired.

SUBSEQUENT ADMINISTRATIONS

Remarkably little has changed in the past twenty years. For a variety of reasons, no administration has undertaken a fundamental reevaluation of the policies as they have existed since the Kennedy presidency.

It is true that each succeeding administration has reviewed doctrine for the use of strategic nuclear forces. Each review has begun with the new civilian leaders erroneously believing that American strategic forces are targeted primarily at Soviet cities. Each review has concluded that additional flexibility was needed and has directed the military to develop additional options for the use of strategic forces. But one fundamental assumption was never questioned: The United States should be prepared to initiate a strategic nuclear exchange. In addition, there has been no review of the proposition that the United States should initiate the use of tactical nuclear weapons whenever "necessary" to avoid defeat on the battlefield.

Thus, America continues to threaten the first use of nuclear weapons and to maintain plans to use such weapons whenever it is deemed in its interest to do so. In particular, the first-use threat—whether on the battlefield, wherever it might be in the world. or directly against Soviet territory—has remained a key component of U.S. policy. During the Carter administration, the United States did state directly that it would not use nuclear weapons first against nonnuclear states that were not engaged in aggression supported by a nuclear power. But this commitment still left the United States free to threaten first use in many situations.

The worldwide deployment of nuclear weapons remains in place. The armed forces of the United States throughout the world are equipped either with nuclear weapons or with weapons that could be mated with nuclear devices in a matter of hours. Training and war plans still assume that nuclear weapons will be used when needed to prevent victory by hostile forces. It is important to note, however, that the training and doctrine of the military services, particularly the army, have come to assume that the authority to use nuclear weapons might well not be granted.[28] This is not an unreasonable assumption, given the history of situations in which the United States has threatened to use nuclear weapons, as we will see in the next chapter.

2 THE MYTHOLOGY OF NUCLEAR THREATS

An overwhelming majority of the American public is misinformed about American nuclear policy. Most Americans believe that their nation, as a matter of policy, would never threaten or consider the first use of nuclear devices.[1] Even many knowledgeable observers believe that the United States has not seriously contemplated the first use of nuclear weapons in many years and that it would seriously consider initiating nuclear war only in response to a massive Soviet attack on Europe.

However, within a small group a mythology has grown up over the years around the value of nuclear threats in resolving international crises. Some career civil servants, military officers, politicians, and others who move in and out of high positions in the Pentagon—a group I will refer to collectively as the "national security bureaucracy"—know that the United States has threatened first use on a number of occasions since Hiroshima. Many of these people strongly believe that such threats have been credible and therefore have played a critical role in resolving the crises. Moreover, these national security bureaucrats argue that the United States must continue to make credible threats of first use in order to defend the nation's vital interests in many parts of the world, including not only Europe but also Northeast Asia and the Persian Gulf.

Clearly, this is not the view of the entire national security bureaucracy. In the previous chapter I referred to a core of military officers who question the value of nuclear weapons. There are certainly civilian skeptics as well. And individuals who do give credence to the nuclear threat may hold this view for different reasons or to various degrees. Generally, however, it is fair to say that faith in the utility of nuclear weapons is dominant in national security circles, and that this faith is grounded in the conviction that nuclear threats have been successful in the past and are necessary to deter future Soviet aggression.

Because of this deep-seated faith, the nuclear threat has been issued on nearly twenty occasions since the end of World War II. But the world of the nuclear threat has been a secret one, hidden from review or assessment by the American public. Having carefully examined the available evidence for each of these crises, I have concluded that the perception that nuclear threats have been central to their resolution is exaggerated in some cases and entirely wrong in others. In each instance, the critical variables have been the nature of the security interests at stake, the balance of conventional military weapons, and skillful diplomacy accompanied by a willingness to compromise—not the nuclear threat. The role of diplomacy, in particular, is often undervalued. Immediately following many of these crises, both the United States and its adversary publicly claimed victory; only years later does the American public learn of the secret diplomatic efforts and private "understandings" that undergirded the resolutions of the crises.

It is also important to understand that on those occasions when the possibility of using nuclear devices arose, the intention was not to win a battlefield victory with them but to coerce the political leadership of the enemy. It is true that the Joint Chiefs of Staff and some civilians have on occasion proposed the tactical use of nuclear weapons designed to avoid defeat in a particular battle, but presidents have never supported such use. Rather, the presidents who gave serious consideration to using nuclear devices did so with the same goal Truman had in mind in 1945: to persuade the adversary to sue for peace.

It is impossible to overstate the importance of the bureaucracy's unfounded confidence in the effectiveness of nuclear threats. In my view, this unwarranted faith is the greatest single obstacle to the adoption of a new American nuclear policy that would substantially reduce the possibility of nuclear war. As long as the myth persists, the United States will continue to treat nuclear devices as weapons and, hence, contemplate their first use. I present the following capsule looks at nineteen nuclear crises since the end of World War II for two reasons: first, to show the reader why important elements of the national security bureaucracy believe that nuclear threats are credible and necessary, and second, to persuade the reader that in fact nuclear threats were not critical to the resolution of these crises.

IRAN (1946)

Soon after the Hiroshima and Nagasaki bombs were dropped, the United States encountered the first crisis of the nuclear age, one that is now long forgotten. With unrest in Iran, the Soviets were slow in removing their troops from that country. The West feared that the Communist Tudeh party would seize control of a province, proclaim it an independent state, and receive immediate diplomatic recognition from Stalin. Under this worst-case scenario, Soviet troops would then return to prevent the central government of Iran from reasserting control over the territory.

Against a backdrop of the American nuclear monopoly, the U.S. government moved quickly and decisively on several fronts to deal with this perceived threat. The United Nations Security Council, then under the firm control of Washington, convened in special session. The Soviets were warned of the importance that the West attached to the territorial integrity of Iran. Preparations for military operations were begun.

Years later, President Truman asserted that he had quietly passed an atomic ultimatum to Stalin to get Soviet troops out of Iran. "Stalin then did what I knew he would do," Truman recalled. "He moved his troops out."[2]

But most students of the crisis believe that the tide turned against the Communists because of internal factors in Iran and the strong international reaction. It appears that the leaders of the Tudeh party never intended to declare a separate state or to ask the Soviets to intervene. There is even good reason to believe that no nuclear threat was actually made.[3] But for the national security bureaucracy, Iran became the first crisis to contribute to the myth of the effectiveness of such threats.

BERLIN (1948)

In 1948 Stalin and the West were engaged in growing disagreement about the future of Germany. The Soviet government, which occupied what later became East Germany, slowly built up a blockade around West Berlin. That January Moscow publicly threatened to oust the West from Berlin. Over the following months, Western air, rail, road, and barge traffic was harassed. A limited airlift of supplies into Berlin was begun to offset the partial blockade. On June 24, however, the Soviets imposed a complete surface blockade. Because Berlin was entirely surrounded by the Soviet-controlled section of Germany, this blockade effectively stopped all supplies by ground to the civilian and military population of the city.

Truman was determined to resist. He pressed for agreement from the Pentagon to send an armed convoy down the access road to Berlin. If the Soviets resisted, the convoy, which did not have atomic weapons, would use whatever force was necessary to fight its way into Berlin. Truman believed that Stalin would back down in the face of American determination.

In what was to become a regular pattern, the Joint Chiefs of Staff opposed military action, arguing that the U.S. military was not yet ready for conflict. The Joint Chiefs also objected to another possibility, a massive military airlift of supplies to Berlin. The air force did not want its planes, designed for strategic nuclear bombing, to be used for a civilian resupply mission. Although Truman relinquished the idea of sending an armed convoy to Berlin, he overruled the Joint Chiefs' objections and in late June ordered an expansion of the airlift.

Still in control of the world's only nuclear weapons, Truman also responded in July by ordering the deployment of sixty B–29 bombers, described by the administration as "atomic capable," to Great Britain (and a lesser number to Germany). While the United States would not reveal whether atomic weapons were present in England, the decision to deploy the bombers was well publicized. Truman clearly hoped to invoke the atomic threat to demonstrate American resolve.[4]

To the surprise of many, the airlift proved capable of supplying the minimum needs of the allied military forces and the civilian population of Berlin. Faced with the choice of shooting down American military aircraft or seeing the blockade fail, the Soviets elected the latter. At the same time, the Soviets and the United States showed a willingness to negotiate. As with many other crises in the nuclear age, once the situation heated up and both sides demonstrated seriousness and resolve, direct secret negotiations became possible.

The American and Soviet ambassadors to the United Nations met secretly over a period of weeks in the first intense bilateral negotiations addressing Soviet and U.S. concerns over the future of Germany. Agreements were reached that permitted the Soviets to end the blockade. In another precedent-setting action that would later become commonplace, both sides claimed victory.

Most analysts credited at the time, and still credit, the success of the airlift, coupled with the willingness to negotiate, for bringing the crisis to a satisfactory conclusion. Many people within the national security bureaucracy, however, believed that the deployment of the B–29 bombers and the atomic threat they implied were crucial to Stalin's decision to back down.

KOREAN WAR (1951-52)

On June 27, 1950, when President Truman made the historic decision to commit U.S. military forces to the Korean war, the armed forces were small, ill prepared for combat, and lacking in direct control over nuclear weapons. The initial debates about whether to intervene found the administration divided; Secretary of State Dean Acheson favored intervention, while Secretary of Defense James Forrestal and the Joint Chiefs were opposed. But no one gave serious consideration to the use of nuclear weapons. Apparently, both Acheson and Forrestal simply assumed that any American involvement would be nonnuclear.

It was only after the Chinese entered the war that the U.S. government paid attention to the question of using atomic weapons in Korea. Once again, the deliberations were mostly private, though on one occasion the use of nuclear weapons was discussed publicly and then quickly qualified. At a press conference on November 30, 1950, Truman, responding to a question, suggested that the United States might be planning for the use of nuclear weapons in Korea. The outcry in the Washington was considerable. In Great Britain the backlash was so great that Prime Minister Clement Attlee, whose government was contributing troops to the United Nations command in Korea, immediately flew to Washington to seek assurance that Truman would consult with the allies before using atomic weapons. Truman told Attlee that the United States was not seriously considering their use in Korea.

Although many of the internal documents from this period have now been released, it is still not possible to determine just how seriously the United States considered using atomic weapons or why Truman made the remark he did at the press conference. The military services, still not in possession of the weapons at this point, questioned their utility and did not advocate their use. They believed that the small extant stockpile should be preserved for the defense of Europe.

Truman recognized the political and diplomatic costs of employing atomic weapons and did not contemplate their use on the battlefield in Korea. Rather, he considered and rejected a demonstration attack similar to that on Hiroshima and Nagasaki, with the political aim of persuading China to end its involvement in the conflict and permit United Nations forces to occupy all of Korea. The Chinese could not have known how serious Truman was. In any event, they did not accept American terms for ending the conflict.

KOREA (1953)

Nowhere were the differences between Eisenhower's and Truman's views of nuclear devices more apparent than in the case of Korea. When Eisenhower came to office in 1953, negotiations to end the war had already dragged on for some time. Eisenhower's campaign platform had included a commitment to travel to Korea before taking office and then to end the war quickly. He assured the American people that he had a plan for ending the war and that he would put it into effect immediately.

The plan, which came to light years later, was to threaten to drop atomic bombs on Chinese cities if the negotiations did not quickly lead to an armistice. Administration officials later claimed that such a threat had been passed to the Chinese through the Indian government and its ambassador in Peking. As with the Iran and Berlin situations, many members of the national security bureaucracy believe these threats were instrumental in bringing the war to an end.

But there are a number of reasons to doubt that this is so. In his memoirs, for instance, the Indian ambassador denies that he was ever asked to pass on such a threat and asserts that he did not do so. Additionally, the armistice terms Eisenhower agreed to were not substantially different from those that had been offered to Truman. The decisive shift in the Chinese position was the acceptance of voluntary repatriation of prisoners of war, and, as McGeorge Bundy points out, this shift came shortly after the death of Stalin and *before* the nuclear threats are said to have been made.[5]

The primary impetus for settlement came from the conventional stalemate on the ground; neither side had any hope of unifying Korea by force. But Eisenhower, being a Republican and a great war hero, had more room to maneuver than Truman did. He could accept terms on such issues as prisoner repatriation that Truman could not. The Chinese, knowing that they would have to deal with Eisenhower for at least four years, had every reason to come to terms quickly. Finally, the new Soviet leaders apparently looked for an early end to the war because they wanted to open up the possibility of negotiating with the Eisenhower administration on a range of other issues.

In short, neither the vague Truman threat nor the possibly more explicit one made by the Eisenhower administration altered the position of the Chinese. Nevertheless, this did not prevent the Korean threat from contributing to the myth of the effectiveness of nuclear threats. Indeed, sixteen years later, Richard Nixon would cite this episode and seek to use the same tactic to end the Vietnam war.

QUEMOY AND MATSU (1954)

The year after the Korean War ended, the Chinese appeared to be moving to capture the offshore islands of Quemoy and Matsu, which were held by the Chinese nationalists. The Eisenhower administration publicly committed itself to the defense of the islands. Because the administration's directives turned nuclear weapons over to the military, Pentagon leaders made preparations to use them as the crisis developed. But it soon became clear that the four-star general in the White House was extremely reluctant to commit U.S. military forces to combat. He was also unwilling to use nuclear weapons automatically, even though that is what his directive NSC 162/1 had implied. Eisenhower was to display these same traits in each of the nuclear crises of his presidency.

Despite U.S. fears, the Chinese did not press their military operations and, it now appears, never intended to do so. American air and naval superiority in the area were the primary military factors in resolving the crisis. However, those who believed in the efficacy of nuclear threats added Quemoy and Matsu to the list of successes.

INDOCHINA (1954)

That same year, Ho Chi Minh's Communists were proving increasingly effective in resisting the French postwar effort to maintain its colony in Indochina. This resistance culminated in the siege of the French base at Dienbienphu. Unable to hold out alone, the French asked for American military intervention to prevent a Communist conquest of Vietnam.

The national security bureaucracy responded by drawing up war plans for American military involvement, including the use of nuclear weapons in the vicinity of Dienbienphu to save the base. It was probably the most formal proposal for using nuclear weapons ever developed by the U.S. government. It was approved by the Joint Chiefs of Staff over the objections of the army. In particular, Admiral Arthur W. Radford, chairman of the Joint Chiefs, pressed Eisenhower for its implementation.

The president responded with characteristic caution. He appeared to consider the plan, but attached three conditions, which he was confident would not be met: a formal request from the French for American intervention, a willingness of U.S. allies to join in, and support from congressional leaders. None of Eisenhower's conditions were met by the French, our allies, or the Congress, and the proposal was not implemented. In the process, however, the allies and congressional leaders gained the impression that the United States was serious about its intention to use nuclear weapons if its troops went into combat.

Proponents of such threats have been quick to argue that *if* a nuclear threat had been made, it would have been successful. The fact remains, however, that despite the military plans, a public nuclear threat was not issued.

SUEZ (1956)

In response to the British and French invasion of Egypt in 1956, the Soviet Union issued its only clear public threat to use nuclear weapons. Soviet leader Nikita Khrushchev warned that rockets would fly against the two nations if their forces were not withdrawn from Egypt. It is doubtful that this Soviet threat was anything more than bluster, and that it in any way influenced the actions of the British and French. As McGeorge Bundy points out, the Soviet threat came only *after* U.S. officials had publically stated that America did not support the invasion.[6]

Although the United States opposed the invasion of Egypt, it responded to the Soviet ultimatum by threatening nuclear retaliation. This was, of course, not a threat of first use but of first strategic use; a Soviet nuclear attack on U.S. allies would trigger an American nuclear attack on the Soviet homeland, even if the United States questioned the merits of the allies' action that provoked the Soviet attack.

At the same time, of course, the United States pursued its own efforts—ultimately successful—to force the British and French to withdraw from Egypt.

LEBANON (1958)

Lebanon's chronic political instability first erupted in 1958 following the revolutionary overthrow of the pro-Western Iraqi government. Lebanon's President Camille Chamoun asked that U.S. forces be sent to his country as a demonstration of support for American allies in the region. Responding with uncharacteristic alacrity, Eisenhower agreed to send in a marine unit.

By then, however, American forces were equipped with nuclear weapons. So two questions immediately arose: Should the United States forces bring nuclear weapons ashore? And should they have the authority to use those weapons in their defense? Apparently, the nuclear weapons were left aboard ship, as were dual-capable weapons that could have been used to deliver conventional weapons.[7] As it happened, the marines did not come under fire and were quickly withdrawn.

This episode, although often included in lists of nuclear crises, did not involve an explicit threat to use nuclear devices. It does, however, show how the "nuclearization" of

U.S. forces diminished their effectiveness in conventional operations.

QUEMOY (1958)

The nuclear versus conventional weapons dilemma seriously deepened with the Quemoy crisis later that same year. It was this incident that brought the United States as close as it has ever come to using nuclear weapons. This near use occurred, as in Lebanon, because of the integration of nuclear and conventional forces, not as a result of threats to vital American interests. And it occurred in defense of territory that few Americans would have considered important to U.S. security.

Located more than ninety miles from Taiwan, Quemoy lies just three miles off the coast of the Chinese mainland. By 1958, the Chinese nationalists had moved one-third of their military forces to Quemoy. Beginning in August, the People's Republic of China initiated a sustained bombing of the island. The American intelligence community predicted that the Chinese would invade Quemoy and that the nationalists would be unable to hold out on their own.

Both Eisenhower and Secretary of State John Foster Dulles issued strong statements indicating that the United States would do whatever was necessary to prevent a Communist conquest of the island. The navy was authorized to assist in convoy operations while remaining outside the three-mile zone of territorial water. Other U.S. military forces in the area were substantially increased. Army artillery capable of firing nuclear weapons were rushed to Taiwan. Those in the administration eager to underscore the nuclear threat leaked this news to the press, along with the U.S. intention to use whatever military force was necessary to resist Communist aggression.

Internally, plans to defend Quemoy were dusted off and updated. These plans, approved by the Joint Chiefs of Staff, assumed that nuclear weapons would be used if U.S. military forces participated in operations in the Taiwan Straits, where

Quemoy is located. In meetings with the president, the Joint Chiefs pressed for approval of these plans and for advance authority to use nuclear weapons. This Eisenhower refused to give. He authorized the use of American forces in the defense of Quemoy but directed that the initial defense involve conventional forces only.

Substantial dispute remains as to how close Eisenhower came to authorizing the use of nuclear weapons. There is no doubt that he hoped to end the crisis without involving American military forces. He pressured the Chinese nationalists to resupply Quemoy (which they did not do, hoping to draw the United States into the conflict militarily) and negotiated with the People's Republic for a peaceful solution. However, the question of what would have happened had the Chinese invaded Quemoy remains unanswered.

Eisenhower's sympathizers maintain that, in the end, he would not have authorized the use of nuclear weapons. If a conflict had begun, they suggest, he would have moved quickly to terminate it, while withholding the authority to use nuclear weapons.

However, internal documents of the time, including those kept by the Joint Chiefs of Staff, tell a very different story. The Joint Chiefs told Eisenhower that they could not defend Quemoy successfully without using nuclear weapons—that they did not wish even to begin the operation without the assurance that the use of nuclear weapons would be authorized. A conventional U.S. defense, in their judgment, would collapse very quickly.

In response, according to the Joint Chiefs' files, the president asked whether there would be time after hostilities began to seek his approval to use nuclear weapons. Told that there would be, Eisenhower decided to withhold nuclear authority. The Joint Chiefs' documents suggest that if the Chinese had launched an invasion, American forces on the scene would have returned fire with the expectation that they would soon have permission to use the nuclear weapons they possessed.

Nuclear threats were conveyed to Peking, and the feared invasion did not take place. To those who see nuclear threats as an effective tool of diplomacy, this correlation is evidence of success. A careful review of the crisis, however, indicates that the Chinese had never intended to invade. The Chinese recognized that Quemoy was more valuable as a hostage; capturing it would have made an invasion of Taiwan, ninety miles off the coast, virtually impossible. The nationalist strategy of not resupplying Quemoy was intended to induce American involvement, despite the low likelihood of a Chinese invasion. If the Chinese *had* attacked Quemoy, the United States might have used nuclear weapons.

BERLIN (1959)

In 1959 the relative tranquility along the border between NATO and the Warsaw Pact was shattered by a Soviet ultimatum demanding a European settlement and warning of a blockade of Berlin. Ultimately, Khrushchev agreed to delay consideration of the issue until a new American administration was installed. However, while the outgoing Eisenhower administration was confronted with this problem, military planners continued to assume that nuclear weapons would be used if they were necessary to maintain access to Berlin.

BERLIN (1961)

Upon taking office, the Kennedy administration inherited the Soviet ultimatum regarding Berlin. This threat to use force in Europe came just as the new administration was moving away from automatic use of nuclear weapons and seeking to improve NATO's conventional military capability. For those who advocated greater reliance on conventional military power, contingency planning for the defense of Berlin posed the most difficult problem in Europe.

Berlin lay deep within East Germany. The Allied garrison in the city simply could not hold out if Soviet forces in Germany launched a full-scale attack on the western sector of the city. If the Soviets imposed a new blockage, Allied military forces might not have been able to ensure access to West Berlin. No conceivable increase in NATO forces in the European theater could change these stark facts.

One possible Allied response would have been to threaten that NATO would launch a conventional military attack against the East. The possibility of becoming embroiled in a large-scale conventional war might have been sufficient to deter any Soviet move. This option, however, was not acceptable to European leaders. They urged NATO to rely on nuclear threats.

The Kennedy administration was skeptical of the utility of a nuclear strategy in defending Berlin. If the Allies launched a nuclear attack on the East, the Allied garrison in West Berlin would be annihilated by the Soviet response, whether nuclear or conventional. Nor would nuclear devices be effective in maintaining a flow of supplies to the population of Berlin. In the administration's view, nuclear devices could be used only to destroy the territory along the supply routes.

Searching for an alternative, American planners returned to the tactic of using nuclear devices as a demonstration of resolve. If the Soviets exerted force to take Berlin, the United States would first respond with conventional forces. The hope was that the Soviets would back down and negotiate after realizing that the West was indeed prepared to fight. If this failed, a nuclear device would be fired—not to influence the local battle but as an attempt to scare the Soviets into withdrawing. If this effort failed, then the only option left would be a large-scale nuclear attack. At the same time, the administration was conducting negotiations at various levels with the Soviet Union, both to communicate the West's resolve and to probe for a diplomatic solution.

The Soviet ultimatum was never implemented. It is impossible to know how much the explicit threat to use nuclear devices, and the contingency planning for such use, affected the Soviet decision. It is certain, however, that proponents of the nuclear threat viewed the outcome as another successful application of their strategy.

CUBAN MISSILE CRISIS (1962)

The Cuban Missile Crisis is generally regarded as the incident that brought the world closest to nuclear war.

On October 16, 1962, President Kennedy learned that the Soviets, over a period of several months, had placed medium- and intermediate-range missiles, equipped with nuclear warheads, in Cuba. The Kennedy administration insisted that they be removed. After considering a range of options during a tense week of secret meetings, President Kennedy announced a blockade of Cuba in an address on October 22, 1962, and clearly indicated that the blockade would be followed up with whatever action was necessary to secure the removal of the missiles. In that speech, Kennedy explicitly warned that if any nuclear-armed missiles were fired from Cuba at any target, the United States would respond with a full-scale nuclear attack against the Soviet Union.

Although we do not know whether the American ships blockading Cuba were authorized to use nuclear weapons, contingency planning for an invasion of Cuba did anticipate a nuclear attack. As the crisis wore on, the administration indicated to the Kremlin, by deeds and private communication, that an invasion was imminent. U.S. forces armed with nuclear devices were placed on alert worldwide.

As I noted above, two common characteristics of nuclear crises are that both sides claim victory and that secret negotiations take place whose results are not made public until years later. The Cuban Missile Crisis was no exception. For years, most Western analysts viewed the outcome of the crisis as a clear victory for the United States. Debate has focused on the relative importance of America's overwhelming conventional superiority in the Caribbean Basin and American nuclear superiority in this victory. It is now clear, however, that diplomatic compromise was at least as important in bringing the crisis to an end as either of these military factors.

At the same time that the United States was issuing nuclear threats, Attorney General Robert Kennedy was also engaged in urgent and secret negotiations with Soviet Ambassador Anatoly Dobrynin aimed at satisfying the interests of both nations and avoiding war. As a result of these negotiations, the United States agreed to withdraw its missiles from Turkey, so that neither superpower would have intermediate-range missiles situated within reach of the other's territory. Another element of the arrangement was that the American commitment to withdraw its missiles from Turkey would not be described as part of the deal.

Thus, many factors combined to induce Khrushchev to remove the missiles from Cuba: diplomatic concessions, American resolve to use force if necessary, the vast U.S. conventional superiority in the region, and American nuclear superiority. It is impossible to assess the relative importance of each factor precisely. It is fair to say, however, that Kennedy's closest advisers during the crisis, and most subsequent analysts, would assign little weight to the role of American nuclear superiority in making the Soviets back down.

Indeed, in light of the new knowledge of the American concessions in Turkey, it is unclear whether the Soviets did in fact "back down." McGeorge Bundy, then Kennedy's national security adviser, argues that the Cuban Missile Crisis showed that all political leaders are extremely reluctant to initiate the use of nuclear weapons and, in so doing, reduced the credibility of all nuclear threats.[8] Nonetheless, influential members of the national security bureaucracy maintain that the Cuban Missile Crisis is one of the clearest examples of using the nuclear threat to make the Soviets "blink."

PUEBLO SEIZURE (1968)

Only fleeting thought was given to the use of nuclear devices in the *Pueblo* incident. When the North Koreans seized an American boat equipped with electronic spying equipment and towed it to shore, the U.S. national security bureaucracy immediately began considering a variety of options to recover the ship, including issuing nuclear threats against North Korea. However, President Johnson stated that his primary goal was to secure the release of the crew unharmed and that he would not consider military options until all efforts at diplomacy had failed. Ultimately, the crew was released after the United States signed an apology.

The extensive nuclearization of American forces did affect the United States response to the crisis in one noteworthy way. Despite the emphasis the Kennedy and Johnson administrations placed on improving conventional capability, the military services continued to give priority to developing and maintaining nuclear capability. As a result, all American planes in the Far East that were on "strip alert"—ready for instant use—during the *Pueblo* crisis were on nuclear alert. This meant that they were capable of taking off and dropping nuclear bombs immediately but not of employing conventional military power quickly.

Thus, when the military commanders in the Pacific learned that an American ship had been seized by the North Koreans and was being towed into port, they could not respond. On the one hand, they had the authority to use conventional force to prevent capture of the ship, but they had no conventional forces on alert and so could not get planes or ships to the scene in time. On the other hand, nuclear weapons were readily available, but they could not be used without presidential authority.

Had conventional forces been on alert in the Pacific, they could have been used to prevent the American ship from being forced into a North Korean port. But no known changes were made in the composition of the forces on alert as a result.

VIETNAM (1968)

The only time the Johnson administration appears to have considered using nuclear devices was in response to the Communist siege of Khe Sanh, a marine base close to the border between North and South Vietnam.

By the time of the Johnson administration, public opinion had turned very quickly against an aggressive nuclear policy, to the point where Johnson found it politically advantageous to discredit the pronuclear stance of his 1964 Republican opponent, Barry Goldwater. When a Goldwater supporter had called for the use of nuclear weapons in Vietnam, Johnson instantly seized the issue. "Make no mistake," he argued. "There is no such thing as a conventional nuclear weapon."[9]

Despite the continuing frustrations of the war, the administration did not consider using nuclear weapons until the marine garrison at Khe Sanh appeared in danger of being overrun. Parallels to Dienbienphu were drawn in public. The administration feared that the humiliation of a marine unit being forced to surrender might end the already flagging U.S. public support for the war. Under these circumstances, military planners considered every option, including the use of nuclear weapons. Finally, however, the administration overwhelmed the Communist siege with conventional air power.

VIETNAM (1969)

Richard Nixon has always aligned himself with those in the national security bureaucracy who believe in the efficacy of nuclear threats. In particular, he believes that President Eisenhower's threat to use nuclear weapons was crucial in bringing the Korean War to an end.

Nixon campaigned for the presidency in 1968, as Eisenhower had in 1952, with the promise of a secret plan to end the war. It was the same plan: a nuclear threat. Nixon explained it to a meeting of southern delegates at the Republican convention, which he believed was off the record but that was, in fact, tape-recorded. This is what he said:

> How to bring a war to a conclusion? I'll tell you how Korea was ended. We got in there and had this messy war on our hands. Eisenhower let the word out—let the word go out diplomatically—to the Chinese and the North Koreans that we would not tolerate this continued ground war of attrition. And within a matter of months they negotiated.

As Nixon told *Time* magazine in July of 1985, upon taking office he considered and rejected the tactical use of nuclear weapons in Vietnam.[10] What he did not report was that the

Nixon administration warned both the Russians and the Chinese that the United States would use nuclear weapons to destroy North Vietnam if it did not accept a negotiated settlement of the war. It is not known whether the Russians or Chinese believed these threats or passed them on to the Vietnamese. We do know that Henry Kissinger later issued such threats directly to the Vietnamese. In any event, nuclear devices were never used in Vietnam, and the ground war dragged on for years.

The official documents reporting these threats have yet to be made public. When they are, they will surely undermine much of the faith in the efficacy of nuclear threats. Vietnam was perhaps the most spectacular failure of a nuclear threat in the entire post-World War II era.

SOVIET-CHINESE CONFLICT (1969-70)

As Nixon reports in the same *Time* interview, sometime during the first two years of his administration, the Soviet government quietly informed the United States that it was considering a nuclear strike intended to destroy the small Chinese nuclear capability. Apparently, the Soviets wanted to know whether the United States would support such action in the name of nonproliferation, remain neutral, or intervene in some way on China's behalf.

After consultation with Nixon, Henry Kissinger, then the national security adviser, warned of the possibility of U.S. nuclear retaliation if the Soviets were to take such an action. It is not known how serious the Soviets were or what role this American threat played in persuading them against acting. As in the Suez situation, the Soviets threatened first use, and the Americans reciprocated with a threat of initiating a nuclear attack on Soviet territory, or first strategic use.

INDIA-PAKISTAN

The United States did not intervene when the Indian government invaded what was then east Pakistan and helped to set up the independent state of Bangladesh. (East and west Pakistan were united politically but separated geographically by India.) However, based on information from sources within the Indian government, the Nixon administration came to fear that India would move into west Pakistan as well.

Perceiving a threat to an ally, the United States responded by moving a large naval force into the Bay of Bengal off the coast of India. The obvious threat was that the United States would intervene militarily if the Indians attacked west Pakistan. Since the fleet was equipped with nuclear weapons, and since it had little effective conventional capability to prevent an Indian invasion, some observers have viewed this action as constituting an implicit nuclear threat.

In his *Time* interview, Nixon said he feared that an Indian invasion of west Pakistan would prompt the Chinese to intervene, which would, in turn, trigger a Soviet response. If this chain of events transpired, he asserted, the United States would have used nuclear weapons against the Soviet Union. However, most serious students of the region believe that the Indians never intended to invade west Pakistan.

ARAB-ISRAELI WAR (1973)

The most celebrated nuclear crisis of the Nixon presidency came during the Yom Kippur War in 1973. After an initially successful attack across the Suez Canal, the Egyptian army had been pushed back, and its key elements were in danger of being surrounded and forced to surrender by the Israelis. In a series of increasingly strident messages and conversations, the Soviet government, then allied with Egypt, stated that it would not tolerate the destruction of the Egyptian army.

When cease-fire agreements were repeatedly violated, Egypt's President Anwar Sadat called for U.S. and Soviet troops to enforce a cease-fire. In a message delivered by U.S. Ambassador Anatoly Dobrynin, the Soviet government informed the United States that "if you find it impossible to act jointly with us in the matter, we should be faced with the necessity urgently to consider the question of taking appropriate steps unilaterally."[11] American intelligence reports confirmed that Soviet airborne troops appeared to be on the move and suggested that they might be equipped with nuclear weapons. The U.S. government was unwilling to see the introduction of Soviet troops under any circumstances.

The United States responded in several ways. It urged restraint on the part of the Soviet Union. It placed its forces on an increased alert status. It persuaded Sadat to withdraw his request for a U.S.-Soviet force and, instead, call for an international United Nations peacekeeping force. Finally, it exerted enormous pressure on the Israeli government to cease its military operations and permit the Egyptian army to escape. This last action was successful and was primarily responsible for defusing the crisis and obviating Soviet intervention. Public attention, however, focused on the military alert, which included U.S. nuclear forces.

Hours after ordering the alert, Nixon warned Soviet leader Leonid Brezhnev that the United States "must view your suggestion of unilateral action as a matter of gravest concern, involving incalculable consequences."[12] The explicit American threat was to send in its own ground forces and not necessarily to use nuclear weapons. Though advocates cite this episode as another example of the successful use of a nuclear threat, in fact no explicit threat to use nuclear weapons had been made. The truth was that the United States yielded to the Soviets' key demand and, through diplomatic means, forced Israel to accept a cease-fire.

This episode revealed that the American public and even the White House itself did not completely understand the U.S. military's alert procedures. Nixon reportedly ordered that the alert be kept secret, not recognizing that a series of alert actions by American forces throughout the world would become known quickly.

The incident also revealed that the military was not capable of alerting only the conventional forces. The United States did have the option, which it rejected, of an alert involving only forces in one region or one command. But the military lacked plans to exclude all nuclear forces from alerts, regional or global. In this instance, even Strategic Air Command and nuclear submarine forces were placed on alert.[13]

In fact, all three of the most recent worldwide alerts ordered by the United States—in 1960 (at the time of the collapse of the summit), 1962, and 1973—inevitably involved nuclear forces and even included those forces designed *solely* for the delivery of nuclear weapons. Thus, in each case, a conventional crisis quickly became a nuclear one, and the risk of nuclear war escalated accordingly.

KOREA (1975)

In 1975 American leaders were concerned about the Vietnam precedent. There, the United States had permitted the North Vietnamese government to overrun South Vietnam. The Ford administration feared that the North Korean government would now expect a similar American response to an attack on South Korea. U.S. leaders also worried that the threat of conventional intervention would lack credibility because of the perceptible war-weariness of the American people in the aftermath of Vietnam. Hence, the decision was made to issue an explicit nuclear threat.

In a press conference on June 20, 1975, Secretary of Defense James R. Schlesinger revealed officially for the first time that the United States had nuclear weapons stored in Korea. He warned the North Koreans that the United States would use these weapons if necessary to defend Korea.

Subsequent news reports confirmed the presence of ground combat nuclear weapons in Korea and pointed out that the use-them-or-lose-them dilemma existed there as well as in Europe. The weapons were stored relatively close to the border and stood in potential danger of being overrun in the event of a surprise attack. However, there is no way to know whether the North Koreans were considering the possibility of an attack and, if so, how they reacted to the nuclear threat.

PERSIAN GULF (1980, 1981)

In response to increased tension in the Persian Gulf, both the Carter and Reagan administrations examined America's ability to move military forces into the region. Both were concerned that U.S. conventional capability was not sufficient to defeat a Soviet military move to seize control of the region's oil reserves. Both administrations announced that they were ready to use nuclear weapons to stop a Soviet military move into the region.

In his State of the Union address on January 23, 1980, President Carter made one of the few explicit threats of nuclear first use issued by an American president. Carter stated that the United States would use "any means necessary" to defeat a Soviet military move into the Persian Gulf area. In his memoirs, he confirms that he intended the speech to be a nuclear threat and that he believes the Soviet leaders got the message.[14]

Two weeks after taking office in 1981, in keeping with Carter administration policy, President Reagan called for an American presence in the Persian Gulf.

> What is meant by a presence is that we're there enough to know, and for the Soviets to know, that if they make a reckless move, they would be risking a confrontation with the United States. . . . [I]t's based on the assumption, and I think a correct assumption, that the Soviet Union is not ready yet to take on that confrontation which could become World War III.[15]

We do not know whether the Soviet leaders have ever contemplated a military move into the Persian Gulf, nor how they evaluated these threats. But many within the national security bureaucracy consider the Persian Gulf to be one of the key areas where the American first-use threat is vital to the security interests of the United States.

A review of these nineteen nuclear crises shows that an influential core within the national security bureaucracy has drawn a very different set of lessons from these incidents than have other analysts and students of each crisis. The vast disparity between their conclusions has important implications for American nuclear policy and for the risk of nuclear war.

Nuclear-threat proponents within the national security bureaucracy derive three main conclusions from these cases.

First, they believe that nuclear threats have been, and continue to be, effective not only in deterring the use of nuclear weapons but also in preventing conventional attacks.

Second, the ability to make credible nuclear threats to deter nonnuclear threats—that is, the first-use threat—is essential to the security of the United States.

And third, the credibility of nuclear threats requires the integration of nuclear devices into the military force posture and the development of plans for fighting wars with nuclear weapons.

Because they draw these conclusions, the military services regularly plan for the use of nuclear devices as weapons and build forces for the delivery of these weapons. Presidents and senior officials still threaten to use nuclear devices from time to time. Nuclear use is implicit in any crisis when U.S. forces go on alert. American policy still rests on the belief that in various circumstances the United States must be ready to use nuclear weapons in a first strike.

In reviewing these same nineteen cases, however, I have tried to demonstrate that the proper lessons to learn are very different. Only if our leaders come to accept this alternative set of lessons will it be possible to alter in fundamental and critical ways the nuclear policy of the United States. The lessons I draw are these.

First, nuclear weapons have never been central to the outcome of a crisis. Rather, the outcome of a crisis is primarily determined by the will and determination of each participant, the strategic interests of the two sides, the conventional military balance, and skillful negotiations combined with a willingness to compromise. Indeed, in many of the situations that the national security bureaucracy views as instances of successful nuclear threats, such threats may never even have been conveyed to the adversary.

Second, presidents have given serious consideration to initiating the use of nuclear devices only when such use is designed to end the conflict by coercing the enemy. They have not considered first use to defeat an enemy force on the battlefield.

Third, nuclear threats are most credible when issued to a state that does not have nuclear devices and when the threat is intended to prevent that government from acting.

Fourth, as presidents have repeatedly refused to authorize the use of nuclear devices, the credibility of the nuclear threat has eroded.

Fifth, the integration of nuclear devices with American military forces inhibits the flexibility and effectiveness of U.S. conventional forces.

And finally, this integration actually increases the risk of nuclear war in a crisis.

Acceptance of these lessons would lead to a new and more effective military posture. In the next chapter, I will explore alternative policy options for dealing with American nuclear devices by focusing on two key questions. First, Under what circumstance should the United States plan to use such devices? And second, How should these devices be integrated into the American military establishment?

3 THREE MODELS OF NUCLEAR FORCES

As the preceding chapters suggest, the nature of U.S. nuclear policy has important consequences for the likelihood of nuclear war and for America's ability to promote its own security. However, the United States need not maintain the nuclear posture that has been built up over the past forty years. It has choices. As I see them, the three "models" of nuclear policy currently available to the United States are:

1. Treating nuclear weapons as "regular weapons" to be integrated into all military planning, as they were at the beginning of the Eisenhower administration.

2. Treating nuclear weapons as "special weapons" whose first use should be carefully considered, a model that, in some form, has been American nuclear policy since the Kennedy administration.

3. Treating nuclear weapons as "explosive devices" that may, under certain very extreme circumstances, be used to demonstrate national resolve but never as weapons to fight wars.

I believe that the third model is a viable option that the United States could adopt unilaterally, without compromising national security. By laying out each option and its policy consequences in this chapter, I hope to show that the explosive devices option must be given due consideration in the U.S. nuclear policy debate.

REGULAR WEAPONS

The regular weapons model rests on a simple assumption embedded within NSC 162/1, approved by President Eisenhower in 1953—that nuclear devices are simply better weapons that may be used as a matter of course in any military conflict.

This model specifically rejects the notion that because nuclear weapons are more destructive, there is something qualitatively different about them. A proponent of the regular weapons posture would point out that the smallest nuclear devices have less destructive power than the largest TNT bombs, and nuclear weapons are more efficient in destroying their targets. Thus, there is a simple, quantifiable continuum of destructive power; the right weapon should be used for each military task without regard to the form of energy providing its destructive capability.

From this perspective, nuclear devices can be used just as other weapons are used. If employed on the battlefield, they can be used to defeat an enemy force. They can hold territory and drive back enemy military units. Even if both sides employ nuclear weapons, their use can be limited to the battlefield. A two-sided nuclear war could be "winnable"— that is, it could end with one side defeating the other on the battlefield, without the larger-scale destruction of their societies. Lastly, because nuclear devices are simply weapons, the threat of initiating their use is a credible and robust deterrent. Threats to use nuclear weapons are simply threats to fight, and thus they are at least as effective as other threats to use force.

A key assumption in this model is that the use of nuclear devices could lead to a more favorable outcome than the United States would achieve in a nonnuclear war. Put another way, a war the United States might lose without using nuclear weapons might be won if nuclear weapons were employed. Underlying this assumption is another assumption, that the Soviet Union, or the Communist bloc, possesses a superior conventional military power that is inherent and immutable. Because the Soviet Union is a totalitarian state with a large population and land mass, it will always be able to field effective conventional military forces anywhere around its periphery. The Western alliance, comprised of democratic states dependent on popular support, will never be able to match this conventional power.

Many explanations have been put forth of how the use of nuclear devices in a war would overcome the perceived Communist advantage in a nonnuclear conflict. Some supporters of the regular weapons model simply make an axiomatic assertion: Nuclear devices are America's most powerful weapons, and therefore they must be our most valuable weapons. Others offer specific "military" rationales. Among them: Nuclear conflict favors democratic nations because their military leaders function better in a fluid situation than do Communist bloc leaders; the use of more powerful nuclear devices will compensate for shortages in manpower; and the threatened use of nuclear devices would deter the adversary from massing its forces for a conventional attack, an action that would create inviting targets for nuclear bombs. Still others argue more vaguely that a nuclear threat raises the stakes and hence makes an attack less likely.

The basic policy implication of this model is that the United States should treat nuclear devices as if they were regular weapons in every possible way. A natural extension of this implication is that the United States should also do all it can to persuade the rest of the world to accept this view and to reject the notion that the use of these devices raises special moral or prudential issues.

In applying this model, the United States would design and deploy its delivery systems to optimize their capability to deliver nuclear devices. Airplanes and short-range missiles should be developed with the assumption that their function will be to deliver nuclear weapons. Alternative bomb racks, which would permit the delivery of conventional weapons, should be discarded. All American military forces throughout the world should be equipped in this way, and their training should assume that nuclear forces would be used in any military operation. All war plans should also be based on this assumption and should provide for the possibility of engaging in sustained combat only with nuclear forces. Even security commitments to foreign nations should be evaluated from this perspective. Such commitments could be given and maintained if—and only if—U.S. military forces could use nuclear devices to deter or defeat an attack.

The public policy implications of this model are quite clear. The United States should do everything that it can to avoid the stigmatization of nuclear devices. Its public statements should describe nuclear devices as weapons to be used in warfare, just as other weapons are used. The United States should condemn first use of force and aggression but not the particular weapons that might be used in the fighting. It should emphasize that its major policy objective is to deter war and that to do so the nation should be prepared to use all of the weapons at its disposal. Efforts to treat nuclear weapons as if they were different from other weapons must be denounced as tactics that undermine the U.S. deterrent and lay the West open to the Soviet superiority in conventional forces.

Arms control policy should reflect the same objectives. The United States should propose measures aimed at reducing the risk of war in general but not measures that single out nuclear weapons for special treatment. This means proposals for nuclear test bans, nuclear-free zones, no-first-use policies, and bans on production of fissionable material all must be rejected as efforts to stigmatize nuclear weapons. Furthermore, since the armed forces are relying primarily on nuclear devices, any measures that interfere with their ability to manufacture, test, or deploy such weapons anywhere in the world would adversely affect U.S. security interests.

The United States came very close to adopting this model as official policy with the presidential directives issued in the early years of the Eisenhower administration. However, as I have stated earlier, Eisenhower demonstrated reluctance to permit the use of nuclear weapons in particular crises. He also began to discuss a nuclear test ban treaty in response to allied and public pressure. As a result, the United States drifted toward the second model, that which regards nuclear devices as special weapons.

SPECIAL WEAPONS

The special weapons model concedes that nuclear devices cannot be viewed as just another variety of weapons. It argues that they are "special" weapons whose first use must be carefully considered.

This model assumes that even the limited use of nuclear devices could escalate to general war and lead to the destruction of the United States and the territory of any country on which they are used. Therefore, the United States should not use nuclear weapons automatically in any military conflict but should consider their use only as a last resort to stave off defeat on the battlefield. Because this limits the value of the nuclear threat in most situations, the United States must also maintain significant conventional fighting capability in order to maintain the credibility of American commitments, avoid unnecessary nuclear risks, and deal with low-level threats. In this respect, the special weapons model parts company with the regular weapons model.

This model also shares many of the assumptions of the first model, however. It views nuclear devices as weapons that can be used effectively in a military conflict. It assumes that nuclear threats are credible and should be made, particularly to prevent defeat in a conventional war by deterring the massing of troops. It assumes that on some occasions the United States can emerge as the clear victor from a nuclear battlefield that does not destroy the society being defended.

But conflict is inherent in the special weapons model. While it assumes that sometimes the United States can and should win a war without nuclear help, it also assumes that in other cases the use of nuclear devices would permit the

United States to avoid defeat in an ongoing war that it was in danger of losing.

Thus military planning and deployment must serve two masters, one nuclear and one nonnuclear, who are frequently at odds. Sometimes the United States might choose to fight with conventional forces only or may be forced to do so by political or diplomatic pressure (as has been the case in every conflict since 1945). Nonetheless, nuclear devices must at all times be integrated into the regular military forces if the threat to use them first is to remain credible. Moreover, since the Soviet Union has tactical nuclear weapons deployed with its forces, the United States must be ready at least to respond in kind to Soviet initiation of nuclear warfare.

Thus, weapons systems must be able to deliver both nuclear and conventional weapons, rendering their design less than optimal to deliver either. Forces in the field must be equipped with both, which increases costs and decreases mobility. Training must take account of both, which reduces the likelihood of comprehensive training in one or the other. The design of war plans must also include both possibilities, and, since it may be necessary to use nuclear devices anywhere in the world, all American forces must be given this dual capability. The knowledge that a conventional conflict may soon shift to one involving nuclear devices may lead a military commander to withhold a portion of his artillery or aircraft for nuclear missions and make other decisions that may debilitate conventional defense efforts.

Because supporters of the special weapons model are of two minds about how they want the world to view nuclear devices, the inherent ambiguities of this model are revealed most clearly in the public statements and arms control positions that accompany adoption of such a policy.

Statements that stress the destructive power of nuclear devices reflect an understanding of the dangers of nuclear warfare to the United States, but they can also undermine the credibility of the American threat to initiate their use and make it very difficult to use nuclear devices as weapons when necessary. On the other hand, assertions of the need to rely on nuclear weapons can stimulate public fears, create diplomatic problems, and interfere with efforts to persuade allies to develop effective conventional forces.

By the same token, efforts to control nuclear devices could help reduce the risk of nuclear war. However, the adoption of any particular proposal tends to stigmatize nuclear weapons and may interfere with specific measures to make nuclear threats a more credible deterrent to conventional attacks. As I will discuss below, this ambiguity of the special weapons model has led directly to official U.S. ambivalence to the nuclear test ban treaty.

Since the Kennedy administration came into office in 1961, the United States has held some version of the special weapons model as official policy. At some times and in some ways the United States has emphasized the special nature of nuclear devices, and at other times and in other ways it has sought to maintain the credibility of its threat to use nuclear weapons. Consistently, however, the United States has avoided making a clear-cut decision about whether nuclear devices are weapons or not.

NUCLEAR EXPLOSIVE DEVICES

Although the models described above are the only two that have been the subjects of serious policy debates over the past thirty years, they are not the only models that should be considered in determining how to safeguard American national security in the nuclear age. There is another possibility—a third model.

It assumes that any attempt to use nuclear devices will introduce a high risk of uncontrollable escalation, leading to the complete destruction of the country in which the war is being fought. Thus, nuclear devices, while vital to American national security, cannot be regarded as weapons and should not be placed in the hands of the military.

There is no question that so long as other nations have nuclear devices, the United States must maintain an arsenal of such devices for use in retaliation. However, if an opponent were to use nuclear weapons on the battlefield, the

United States should not respond in kind; to do so would only destroy the country on whose soil the war was being fought. This country would very likely be a U.S. ally, particularly if the war took place in Europe.

There is considerable evidence that nuclear devices cannot be used successfully and in a limited manner on the battlefield. For the past forty years, the military services and a number of civilian analysts have attempted to develop a militarily effective means of using nuclear devices as weapons without destroying the battlefield and the surrounding area. But no one has succeeded. Most war games in which nuclear weapons have been used have escalated very rapidly to all-out nuclear war between the superpowers.

If an opponent were to use nuclear weapons on the battlefield, the appropriate U.S. response would be to use, or threaten to use, nuclear devices against targets of great value to that opponent. To respond on the battlefield would merely increase the chance of global nuclear war; to respond with a threat beyond the battlefield would slow the process of retaliation and demonstrate to the enemy that America seeks a quick end to the conflict.

The fundamental assumption underlying the other models is that the United States and the West together cannot match the Soviets in manpower and conventional capability and in compensation must rely on the first use (or threat of first use) of nuclear devices as weapons. This is an assumption that the third model does not accept.

First, it is not a foregone conclusion that the United States and its allies would necessarily be at a disadvantage in a conventional war with the Soviet Union anywhere in the world. The Soviets are not invincible; they need to be concerned about the weaknesses of their military forces, the unreliability of their allies, and the possibility of attacks from a number of other adversaries, most significantly China. In any case, the Soviets are unlikely to attack in Europe or elsewhere unless they possess a clear conventional advantage *and* strong political incentive to do so—neither of which is evident today or in the foreseeable future.

Second, rather than preventing an enemy from massing his troops, as many argue, the use of nuclear devices is just as

likely to facilitate an offensive breakthrough. The high
casualty rate that would inevitably accompany even a battlefield nuclear exchange would put a premium on sheer numbers of military personnel, thereby increasing, rather than
decreasing, the importance of the Soviet advantage in manpower.

And third, as I explained above, there is a high probability that the use of a single nuclear device would trigger escalation to general nuclear war, which could well destroy the
planet. For this reason, many advocates of the third model,
including me, argue that "the United States should base its
military plans, training programs, defense budgets, weapons
deployments, and arms negotiations on the assumption that
it will not initiate the use of nuclear weapons."[1] In other
words, a no-first-use policy is a natural outgrowth of the
acceptance of the third model.

The model itself does not in all circumstances preclude the
threat of first use nor the actual initiation of nuclear use.
Some proponents of the third model would not rule out
this possibility in extreme circumstances. However, first use
under these circumstances (as well as any retaliatory use)
would proceed on the assumption that nuclear devices are
tools for ending a war, not weapons designed to win a battle.
As Thomas Schelling explains it, the importance of nuclear
devices in this situation is not their tactical capability but

> what they do to the expectation of general war, and what rules or
> patterns of expectations about local use are created. It is much more
> a war of dares and challenges, of nerve, of threats and brinksman-
> ship, once the nuclear threshold is passed. This is because the danger
> of general war, and the awareness of that danger, is lifted an order of
> magnitude by the psychological and military consequences of nu-
> clear explosion.[2]

Against an opponent that has no nuclear capability, the
intent of using nuclear devices would be to frighten the
enemy into surrender by holding out the prospect of the
total destruction of the country under attack; this was the
message of the Hiroshima attack. If used against a country
that possesses nuclear devices of its own, the purpose must be
to demonstrate a willingness to risk the destruction of the

world if the threatening event, presumably a war that one is losing, is not brought a halt. This is what NATO refers to as a "shot across the bow."

Most proponents of the third model, however, believe that no American goal merits running the risk of nuclear war, and they are very skeptical of the value of such a "demonstration." Such an act, they maintain, would frighten the American public, allied governments, and allied populations much more than it would scare hostile governments. And in the midst of a war, the use of nuclear devices would be just as likely to increase pressure on the United States to end the war as it would be to persuade the Soviets to end a war they were winning and return to the status quo. In Europe, given the vulnerability of NATO nuclear forces, a demonstration use of nuclear devices could well engender an all-out Soviet attack on NATO's remaining nuclear forces. This would almost certainly lead to the destruction of Europe, if not the world.

Thus, any effort to offset the consequences of conventional inferiority by relying on nuclear threats is likely to backfire and runs an unacceptable risk of destroying the world. The appropriate response to a perceived conventional weakness is to increase the capacity of conventional forces, not to increase reliance on nuclear devices.

The policy implications of this model are clear. Since nuclear devices cannot be used as weapons, they should not be integrated into the armed forces. Rather, they should be held outside the military structure altogether (as they were by the AEC in the 1940s and as biological weapons were until the Nixon administration eliminated them in 1970), or kept in a separate military service or command whose sole function is to maintain and operate the delivery system for nuclear weapons and to fire the weapons on targets designated by the president at his command.

The military services should proceed as though nuclear devices do not exist. They should develop and deploy their forces, and conduct training and military planning, only for conventional operations. If a war begins, it should be fought on the assumption that nuclear devices are not available. If American military forces in the field come under nuclear attack, the response should be aimed at persuading the adversary's political leaders to bring the war to an end, not at winning the war on the battlefield.

America should assess its commitments to defend allies on the assumption that nuclear devices do not exist and that threats of nuclear first use are unlikely to be effective. The United States and its allies worldwide must determine the level of risk entailed in various relationships of allied forces to Soviet forces, and they must decide whether that risk is worth taking. That choice should be made with two simple propositions in mind: First, the West has the economic resources and the manpower to maintain whatever conventional military balance it determines is necessary. And second, nuclear devices cannot fill the void created by a perceived conventional imbalance.

The stockpile of nuclear devices should be held separately from the regular military forces in the United States or overseas. Any decision to use them should be made directly by the president, who would then release the warheads to the military. Any proposal to initiate their use should be viewed with great skepticism. Plans for retaliating against others who use them should focus first on the president and his closest advisers engaging in a process of careful deliberation and then on employing the nuclear devices in a manner designed to bring the conflict to an end as quickly as possible.

The public pronouncements of the United States should emphasize that nuclear devices are not weapons and that the United States does not believe that they could not be used effectively in combat. Americans would still be in the business of "educating our allies about the realities of the nuclear age," but that process would consist of seeking to convince them that nuclear devices are not instruments of war that can be substituted for conventional military forces. The United States should also seek to convince other nations with independent nuclear capabilities that any effort to use nuclear threats is likely to backfire and, in any case, would lead to their destruction.

Rather than viewing antinuclear movements as a threat, the United States could then consider supporting such efforts around the world. America should not seek to deploy nuclear devices on the territory of any other nation; it should not have nuclear devices aboard ships that seek to call at foreign ports. In addition, the United States should encourage other nations to prohibit the storage of nuclear devices on their territory and forgo independent nuclear capabilities.

U.S. arms control policy should be designed to stigmatize nuclear weapons and endeavor to inhibit their development by the existing nuclear powers and by other nations. Additional testing and production would not be necessary; current warheads would be sufficiently accurate and reliable to demonstrate resolve or retaliate for their use by others. The United States could support a test ban, a fissionable materials production ban, and nuclear-free zones. Moreover, the military services would have no basis on which to object to measures affecting nuclear devices, which would have been removed from their control and planning purview.

To those familiar only with the traditional regular weapons versus special weapons debate over nuclear policy, the explosive devices model might seem utopian or unworkable. But it is not. By breaking free of the conventional assumptions of the national security establishment and rejecting the notion that nuclear devices are weapons, this model allows us to see the nuclear question in an entirely new way. We can then go on to implement this policy with our forces worldwide, without international agreements or Soviet reciprocity, and without compromising American national security, in such a way that the risk of nuclear war is actually lessened and the ability to fight effectively increased.

In implementing this new policy, the American government would need to revamp four elements of the American defense system: strategic nuclear forces, NATO, armed forces elsewhere in the world, and arms control policy. All four have different structures, different histories, and different barriers to change. In the next four chapters, I will carefully lay out a different approach for each.

4 STRATEGIC NUCLEAR FORCES

America's strategic nuclear forces—those forces that would be used in a direct attack on the Soviet Union in a time of hostility—have enormous destructive power. They carry about 3,500 megatons of TNT, only a small fraction of which would destroy the Soviet Union, and perhaps the entire planet. The Soviets have an even larger destructive capacity. In the event of a nuclear war, each side would have the capability to destroy the other many times over; yet neither has the capacity, even in a surprise attack, to wipe out enough of the other's force to ensure its own survival.

The very existence of these forces carries with it some possibility of their use. Even worse, the way in which U.S. and Soviet forces are structured substantially increases this danger. For example, an American president might feel compelled by the vulnerability of nuclear weapons and their command facilities to order the release of the forces before he knows with certainty that the Soviets have launched an attack, or even before the Soviets decide to attack. Similarly, the American force posture, which offers many tempting military targets, might well trigger a Soviet preemptive attack that could eliminate the American ability to respond. Finally, nuclear war might be set off by inadvertent or unauthorized firing of American strategic forces—risks that are greater than they need be due to current U.S. policy and posture.

It may seem surprising that the American strategic force, perhaps the most powerful and destructive military arsenal ever assembled, could be subject to errors, hasty judgments, and attacks launched to exploit its vulnerability. But many aspects of the American strategic nuclear force are surprising. Few subjects have been discussed so often and with so much confusion.

A large part of the confusion arises from a failure to distinguish between the various aspects of "official" policy. It is natural to assume that American policy on the use of nuclear weapons is consistent with declaratory policy (the nation's stated nuclear intentions), targeting policy (which determines what Soviet targets will be attacked in a strategic strike), and policies governing the procurement and development of weapons systems. The reality, however, is that each of these has evolved differently and independently.

A HISTORY OF FALLACIES

The history of American strategic nuclear policy goes back to the air force's doctrine of "strategic bombing," developed for conventional bombs during World War II. When the air force became a separate service after the war, the Strategic Air Command (SAC) was its heart. Through the development of long-range nuclear bombers, SAC acquired the capacity to inflict massive damage on the Soviet war-making capacity, including industry and natural resources.

The SAC war plan, first approved by the Joint Chiefs of Staff in 1950, called for the destruction of Soviet nuclear and other military assets and urban-industrial targets as quickly as possible at the beginning of hostilities—either in response to a Soviet conventional attack in Europe or in anticipation of such an attack. The idea was to strike quickly before the Soviets could consolidate their gains in Europe. As the Soviets developed nuclear devices and bombers to deliver them, those new assets were added to the list of targets, heightening the perceived need to strike quickly and, if possible, to preempt a Soviet attack. This doctrine of preemption is an ongoing element of American strategic planning.[1]

With the growth of the American nuclear stockpile, nuclear devices became available to other parts of the air force as well as to the army and navy. Some of these warheads were stored on both air force and navy airplanes that could reach the Soviet Union. The warheads were assigned to similar types of targets and, in some cases, literally the same targets as SAC bombers already had covered. Yet no effort was made to coordinate the war plans or targets of the various forces.

Even when new strategic nuclear weapons were added to the American arsenal in the 1950s, this basic lack of coordination continued. Intercontinental ballistic missiles (ICBMs) were assigned to the air force and, in turn, to SAC. Medium-range missiles such as Thor and Jupiter, which had a range of 1,200 miles, were assigned to the air force and the army and were under the control of the Supreme Allied Commander Europe. Submarine-launched ballistic missiles (SLBMs) were assigned to the navy and placed under the command of the admiral in charge of the sea in which they were deployed.

The "decisions" to assign these forces to various services and commands were not made by the secretary of defense or the president based on some strategic rationale. Rather, they followed from a "treaty"—known informally as the Key West agreement—negotiated among the military services in 1948. This agreement divided military functions among the services, often allocating weapons systems according to how they operate rather than what their mission is. Thus, missiles fired from the sea belong to the navy even if they have the same function or target as missiles fired from land.[2] Land-based tactical aircraft are under the command of air force generals with responsibilities throughout the world, but tactical aircraft based on navy carriers report to the admiral commanding the waters in which the aircraft carriers sail. This lack of coordination persists largely because forces can be developed only by the service that has authority to deploy them under the Key West agreement—not by the president or secretary of defense.

The development of SLBMs is a good example. Under the Key West agreement, only the navy can build submarines, even if their purpose is to deliver strategic nuclear weapons. No central decision-makers decided that a second system of ballistic missiles was needed to complement the bomber force. Rather, the navy undertook the SLBM program because a small group within that service saw it as a way to strengthen the navy's role in nuclear war planning. Admiral Hyman Rickover, who directed the navy unit that built nuclear reactors, supported the idea, and his team viewed this new system as a challenge and an opportunity. Once the navy built the system, it deployed submarines and assigned them according to its own standard operating procedures.

Ground-based ballistic missiles came to be built largely because scientists developed technologies that were, in the end, "too sweet" to resist. The air force, dominated by flyers, at first had little interest in missiles. It was driven to accept them by the enthusiasm of the scientists and the fear that otherwise the army would lay claim to them. As it was, the air force had to share authority for shorter-range missiles with the army.

Although senior civilian officials supported all of the missile programs, they did so because the technology seemed efficient, not because of an established policy about the need for several different delivery systems or an explicit strategy about how nuclear wars should be planned for or fought. The decisions that produced the "triad" (a nuclear defense system with three legs—bombers, land-based missiles, and sea-based missiles) were all made before the Soviets had any significant capacity to attack the United States. Amazing as it may seem, the policies that guided the Pentagon's procurement and development of strategic weapons were not linked to strategic doctrine.

WAR PLANS: THE SINGLE INTEGRATED OPERATIONAL PLAN

Just as the existing rules determined which services could build various weapons systems, they also dictated how the forces would be deployed. Accords negotiated at the same time as the Key West agreement established the command structures of the military and made control of forces dependent on where the forces are deployed, not on their mission.

When ICBMs were assigned to the air force in the 1950s, SAC coordinated their targets with the targets of its own longer-range bomber force. However, this deployment remained separate from that of army missiles deployed in Europe, which were controlled by the supreme commander there and incorporated into his plans for nuclear operations in the European theater. And when the first navy SLBM system, the Polaris, became operational in the early 1960s, its deployment was not coordinated with the other two services; Polaris subs were assigned to various fleets, and the navy instructed the fleet commanders to determine their targets.

The fact that the forces were under separate command, led to heated debate about how to coordinate nuclear forces, particularly between the navy and the air force. The air force pushed hard for a unified command under its authority. But in 1960, Secretary of Defense Thomas Gates rejected the idea and ordered the air force and the navy to develop a joint war plan for the use of SAC's strategic bombers, the ICBMs, and the SLBMs. In response, the two services designed the Single Integrated Operational Plan for nuclear war, referred to in the national security bureaucracy as the SIOP (pronounced sy-op).

So far as the United States can be said to have a plan for nuclear war, it is the SIOP. But from the beginning, no effort has been made to incorporate other forces that could reach the Soviet Union with nuclear weapons—most significantly, short-range missiles, tactical fighters, and sea-launched surface-ship weapons including cruise missiles (SLCMs) based on aircraft carriers. In fact, the navy was reluctant to accept cruise missiles until it was clear they would not be included in the SIOP. And the forces that were included in the SIOP have never been placed under a single command. They remain deployed under the same separate commands that controlled them before the SIOP was first developed more than twenty-five years ago.

The first SIOP was developed without major civilian input beyond Gates's decision that it should exist. It provided for a single massive strike with all available forces—that is, all the forces included in the SIOP—against military installations and industrial targets in the Soviet Union and the territory of its "allies," including China. In theory, the president would determine whether the forces would be used. However, if he authorized an attack, all the warheads would be launched immediately against all targets. The possibility of undertaking less than a full-scale attack was not considered.

The rationale for this plan was dictated largely by armed services rivalries and U.S. capabilities at the time. Air force doctrine, which dominated American nuclear planning after World War II, held that strategic bombing would win the war, and the navy had no reason to quarrel. Both services considered it important to hit all of the military and industrial targets at once to force a surrender before Soviet ground armies overran Europe. The option of reliably targeting only Soviet strategic forces did not exist since the Soviets had few such forces and the U.S. military did not know their location. Thus only an all-out attack was possible. Under the existing nuclear doctrine of the Eisenhower administration, it was assumed that an all-out attack meant the immediate use of nuclear devices.

The lack of options in the plan reflected not only the military's belief that the forces should be used immediately but also the desire to keep civilians from interfering with the conduct of war. If there were options for using the strategic forces, civilian leaders in the Pentagon and the White House might well want to participate in the decisions after war began.

The SIOP was one of the many issues of contention between the military and the civilian "whiz kids" who came into the government with President Kennedy in 1961. They argued over who should draft it, what it should include, and who should make decisions once a war began. Out of this conflict came a compromise whose basic elements have remained in place: The SIOP is drafted annually by the military and approved by civilian leaders. The extent to which civilians are permitted to review and change the plans remains a matter of dispute to be negotiated anew by each administration.

Over the years, increasingly sophisticated options have been added to the original all-out attack plan. These options permit the exclusion of certain categories of targets, such as particular countries or urban industrial areas. The SIOP also permits the firing of a small number of missiles directed at particular targets. The plan is built on the assumption that in a time of hostilities the president will choose one or more options—at once or in succession—and then leave the military free to execute them.

However, the plan does not provide the president many options about *when* to fire the missiles. It assumes that U.S. strategic nuclear forces will be fired *before* Soviet missiles are fired, before they land on American soil, or, at the very latest, immediately after Soviet missiles reach their targets.

CONFUSING STRATEGY WITH OPERATIONS AND PROCUREMENT POLICY

There is disturbingly little connection between the drafting of the SIOP and the development or deployment of strategic nuclear forces that might be used to carry it out. There is also very little connection between the SIOP and the actual arrangements for how the forces operate. Simply put, the way the system would work in practice is another matter and not the responsibility of those who draft the war plan.

The civilian officials who took on the SIOP and a number of other issues did not seek to alter the basic agreements that assigned forces to the services and dictated command arrangements. For example, although the development of options increased the importance of maintaining centralized control over all the strategic forces, the split command structure was left in place. Orders to execute portions of the SIOP go from the Joint Chiefs of Staff to SAC and separately to the regional commanders, who then pass them on to their naval and air force components. Neither this cumbersome structure nor the problems raised by having strategic forces in two or three services were seriously questioned in 1961 or any time since.

Perhaps the clearest example of the gap between nuclear strategy and operational and procurement policy was the misunderstanding about the mutual assured destruction (MAD) "doctrine" under the Kennedy administration. Faced with the prospect of a Soviet ICBM force for the first time, Secretary of Defense Robert McNamara announced in 1961 a strategy known as "no-cities," which asserted that any United States strategic attack would focus on Soviet strategic forces and would not attack Soviet cities. Soon afterward, however, McNamara made another public statement in which he seemed to lay out an entirely different doctrine. In discussing the question of the size and shape of the American strategic forces, McNamara announced that the United States would maintain forces sufficient to survive a Soviet attack and still permit each leg of the triad—the bombers, the ICBMs, and the SLBMs—to destroy independently some 25 percent of the Soviet population and industry.

However, the "assured destruction" criterion, as it was known in the Pentagon, was not meant as a war plan. Rather, McNamara and his associates adopted the measure because their efforts to develop procurement criteria based on how the United States planned to fight a war had produced no reliable guidelines for determining how much was enough. Seeking a way to control spending on strategic forces, civilians in the Pentagon worked out a criterion that seemed credible and that provided a rationale to reject proposals for building even larger strategic forces.

Critics from the right first pretended not to understand the difference between guidelines for procurement and war plans, and then came to believe that McNamara's speech reflected what the United States in fact planned to do. Labeling the doctrine mutual assured destruction, or MAD, they criticized it as both immoral and ineffective. Critics from the left have argued that the efforts of successive administrations to develop more options in the SIOP simply indicate that American leaders are actively striving to develop the capability for winning a nuclear war.

But both sets of criticisms have missed the point—that planning for the SIOP and procurement and operations policy have proceeded independently. The SIOP has always provided for options other than attacking cities, and the forces procured and deployed by the military services have always given the United States the capacity to attack other kinds of targets. The real fights inside the government about the SIOP continue to focus on how many options there should be, which ones they will be, who should design them, and how they should be executed. Meanwhile, debates about force procurement both inside the government and in public have too often proceeded independently from this war planning debate and have not been geared to providing the forces necessary to meet the criteria in the SIOP.

Despite the changes in the SIOP, the basic structure of the strategic force has not changed significantly since the late 1950s. The United States had then, and has now, a fleet of long-range bombers, ICBMs, and SLBMs. Each part of the force has undergone some modernization. There has been a very substantial reduction in the total megatonnage of the force due to a shift away from bombers, while at the same time the number of separate warheads has increased substantially.

Multiple warheads that can be targeted independently (MIRVs) are now on the missiles deployed on land and at sea. The navy is currently deploying its third-generation submarine and SLBM, and the air force is deploying a new bomber after years of struggle against skeptical civilians. The Minuteman force of 1000 missiles remains the heart of the ICBM force; as of 1987 some 26 larger Titan missiles were being phased out and 50 MX missiles were being built to be placed in Minuteman silos. A small number of medium-range missiles were removed from Europe in the 1960s, and newer cruise and Pershing II missiles were installed in the mid-1980s. Toward the end of the Carter administration, attention turned to improving the command and control system for the strategic forces. During the 1970s, the Carter administration decided to install cruise missiles on bombers and in Europe, and in the early 1980s, the Reagan administration decided to deploy cruise missiles on ships.

One change in the apparent capability of the force stems from the deployment of MIRVs and improvement of accuracy. To the extent that calculations are accurate and systems will work as planned, the United States would, by the end of the 1980s, theoretically have the capacity to destroy most of the Soviet fixed land-based missile force in a first strike, assuming that the Soviets did not launch their force on warning of an attack. The Soviets, who have substantially increased the size and composition of their forces since the early 1960s, already have such a theoretical capability against the American ICBM force but not against U.S. bombers or submarines.

THE CURRENT STRATEGIC NUCLEAR POSTURE

As with the war plans, force structure, and command arrangements, the objectives of the U.S. strategic forces have changed little since the early 1960s. It remains their goal to deter a Soviet nuclear attack on the United States as well as to help deter a massive Soviet conventional attack in Europe.

The nuclear forces capable of attacking the Soviet Union are an integral part of the regular military forces of the armed services. Many are, in fact, dual capable and have both nuclear and nonnuclear warheads, though these are not classified by the Pentagon as part of the strategic force posture. It is unlikely, however, that the Soviets would detect or care about the difference between a strategic nuclear weapon and a tactical nuclear weapon when it is falling on their homeland.

Apart from its enormous destructive power, the most important aspect of the strategic nuclear posture is how it would function in a crisis. In peacetime the emphasis is on negative control—that is, preventing the forces from being fired without authority. With the exception of the submarine missiles, all of the strategic warheads are locked up and cannot be fired without authorization messages, which include the codes for unlocking the weapons. There are elaborate arrangements on the submarines, in the missile silos, and aboard the bombers to ensure that no single person can fire the weapons and that they are not released inadvertently. With the exception of locking up the missiles on the submarines, most observers seem to believe that the United States has done what it can to prevent unauthorized or accidental firing of the strategic nuclear forces in a noncrisis situation.

But the danger increases significantly when a crisis begins. The standard operating procedures of the strategic nuclear forces move from an emphasis on negative control to an emphasis on positive control—that is, to making sure that the weapons will in fact be fired if so ordered rather than ensuring that they will *not* be fired without authorization. And, as I explained in the discussion of the Yom Kippur War of 1973 in Chapter 2, the United States does not have separate alert procedures for conventional and nuclear forces. Alerts have not even separated strategic and tactical nuclear forces. The American military forces are a seamless web and they move up the scale of alert status as one. Thus, as an alert progresses, the conflict between negative control and positive control becomes acute, especially since the communications channels designed to pass orders from the president to the strategic forces are extremely vulnerable to a Soviet attack.

Bruce G. Blair, a former Minuteman launch control officer and a leading expert on strategic command and control problems, cautions that anything said about this subject is affected by the uncertainty that comes from not being able to test the system. In *Strategic Command and Control*, a book stressing the current vulnerability of the command and con-

trol system, Blair describes the trade-off between positive
and negative control as follows:

> The current vulnerability of these networks [for communicating
> orders] creates a particularly knotty problem because it brings posi-
> tive and negative control into sharp conflict. Negative control can-
> not be tightened to a point where all activities of nuclear units re-
> quire the direct personal approval of the president. Not only would
> that degree of centralization be immobilizing, but it would also
> invite a carefully planned attack against the national command
> authority that could neutralize the entire U.S. arsenal. Yet the de-
> centralized arrangements necessary to reduce the risk of such decapi-
> tation and ensure positive control also heighten the risk of acciden-
> tal or unauthorized use of nuclear weapons. Neither centralization
> nor decentralization can eliminate the potential for discontinuity
> between national objectives and force operations.
>
> The inherent tension that exists between the two control priorities
> has created a situation in which they are neither equal nor static.
> In peacetime, negative control is predominant. In wartime, positive
> control takes precedence. Somewhere in between these circum-
> stances a transition occurs. The transition may or may not be cen-
> trally directed, orderly, or complete.[3]

Thus, as a crisis deepens, a president may authorize increased alert status for the military forces without realizing
that he is simultaneously removing the controls on the strategic nuclear forces and actually increasing the likelihood of
their being fired accidentally or without authority. This is
exactly the situation President Nixon encountered during the
Yom Kippur War. Even if a president were to learn of this
problem there would be no way to avoid it at the time,
except by reducing the readiness of the entire military
establishment.

As the U.S. strategic forces move closer to being launched,
the Soviet forces will observe the preparations and may increase their own alert status beyond that ordered because
they perceive increased tension. These moves toward greater
readiness are likely to interact with each other, producing
ever-higher levels of alert until (1) the crisis abates or (2) one
side crosses the threshold into a positive control situation in
which weapons are fired by accident or without authority.

There is, however, a third possibility. In a crisis, the president of the United States or the general secretary of the Communist party of the Soviet Union may decide that a nuclear exchange is so imminent—or, incorrectly, that it is underway—that he orders an attack in the hope of minimizing losses.

The danger of such a preemptive strike is heightened by the fact that both sides have the capacity to destroy a significant portion of the other side's force, and the fragile systems that control them, in a first strike. This possibility is further increased, at least on the American side, by the widespread conviction that it is important to strike as soon after the Soviets launch their attack as possible—assuming the United States does not strike first. Blair starkly described the degree to which this belief permeates the ethos of SAC and the details of the war plans:

> Strategic organizations ... expect to receive retaliatory authorization within minutes after initial detection of missile launchers. That expectation is so deeply ingrained that the nuclear decision process has been reduced to a drill-like enactment of a prepared script, a brief emergency telecommunications conference whose purpose is to get a decision from the national command authority before incoming weapons arrive.[4]

If, in a crisis, intelligence sensors detect a Soviet missile attack on the United States, the president will be told that the missiles are on their way and that he must authorize a response before they land. No doubt he would be pressed to authorize a large-scale response against all legitimate military targets, regardless of the expected civilian damage and before it became known at which targets the Soviet missiles are aimed.

At the same time, Soviet leaders know that American policy calls for the launching of a first strategic strike against the Soviet homeland in response to massive Soviet provocation, such as an attack across Europe, even in the absence of evidence of a Soviet attack on the United States.

Thus, both sides are faced with a situation that Thomas Schelling describes as "the reciprocal fear of surprise attack."[5] Each side, knowing that the other is considering an attack, comes to believe that war is very likely and that the opponent must be preparing to strike. Each is then compelled to consider a strike. These calculations of two rational actors are further exacerbated by the fact that the two systems are moving to an alert status, which increases the likelihood of accidental war and reduces central control over the individual forces.

Each of these characteristics of the current strategic nuclear posture increases the risk of nuclear war. The United States, regardless of Soviet behavior, needs to adopt an alternative posture that reduces those risks.

AN ALTERNATIVE STRATEGIC NUCLEAR POSTURE

The problem with America's strategic nuclear posture begins, as do so many other problems regarding nuclear policy, with the premise that nuclear devices are weapons that should be turned over to the military, who will plan to use them in war. As I argued in the previous chapter, it is entirely possible to reject that premise—and once it is rejected, to see policy options that were previously hidden. If nuclear devices are not weapons, it follows logically that they should not be integrated into the regular military establishment. It also follows that, because strategic nuclear devices are so destructive and their use so unlikely to be limited, the United States should never initiate a strategic nuclear exchange but, rather, use nuclear devices only to deter their use by others.

The application of these principles to the design and deployment of America's strategic nuclear forces would lead to fundamental changes that could substantially reduce the risk of nuclear war without adversely affecting the security of the United States or its allies. Specifically:

1. The United States would design and deploy its strategic forces, and their command and control systems, so that they could survive for a considerable period after a nu-

clear attack and so that they did not pose a threat to Soviet strategic forces.

2. The strategic nuclear capability would be separate from the conventional military forces, except for the NATO nuclear command. The strategic nuclear forces would be subject to a separate chain of command and would be under a single commander, perhaps of a new military service.

3. In a crisis, the nuclear forces would react so as to increase their survivability but not their ability to fire quickly. Presidential directives would indicate precisely that the United States would never fire first and would not fire quickly in response to a Soviet attack.

Design and Deployment

As I explained earlier, the current design and deployment of American strategic nuclear forces does not stem from any single strategic doctrine or concept. It is the result of many influences, including the interests of the individual military services and standard operating procedures. To adopt an alternative nuclear posture, the United States would have to change the process for designing and building the force as well as instructions to the military regarding the purpose of the force.

Currently the strategic forces are intended to present a credible threat that they can be used before the Soviets have fired their strategic forces, yet without stimulating "crisis instability" by creating incentives for both sides to strike first. These goals are incompatible. A credible threat to strike first requires precisely the ability to destroy a significant portion of the other side's strategic forces. That capability, along with the plans to strike first, exacerbates crises by pushing both sides toward a preemptive strike. In addition, it is not possible to assure both that the force will never be used without authority *and* that it would respond quickly to an order to fire.

The model presented here would eliminate these internal contradictions and provide three very clear criteria for the design of the strategic nuclear forces.

The first criterion would be to avoid creating targets that the Soviet Union would be tempted to strike in a crisis. American forces should be deployed so that they simply are not targetable or so that the target they present cannot be destroyed without expending more warheads than are in the target. Submarine-launched ballistic missiles, for instance, cannot be targeted when they are stationed at sea. American nuclear submarines move quietly over vast portions of the ocean floor, and although they have been deployed since the late 1950s, the Soviets still have no reliable capacity to target them. Other nuclear devices that cannot be targeted include nuclear-armed cruise missiles aboard submarines, ballistic missile submarines operating in shallow waters off the coast of the United States, mobile ICBMs, ICBMs in very deep underground silos that would survive even a direct hit, and bombers on airborne alert.

An example of a system that can be targeted, but cannot be destroyed without expending more warheads than are in the target, is a single-warhead ICBM in a hard fixed silo. In order to be certain of destroying the silo, the Soviets would have to fire at least two warheads to destroy the one warhead atop the missile. Thus the Soviets would have little incentive to strike since they would use up more warheads than they destroyed. If, by an arms control agreement or unilateral action, the United States maintained roughly as many warheads as the Soviet Union, the Soviets could not afford so costly an attack.

The second criterion that should guide the design of American strategic forces is that they be capable of destroying only a small portion of the Soviet strategic forces quickly in a first strike. So long as the United States is able to destroy a large fraction of the Soviet strategic force in a first strike, the Soviets face the use-them-or-lose-them temptation that could lead to a preemptive first strike in a crisis. Of course, by designing survivable forces similar to those described above, the Soviets could unilaterally deprive the United

States of that capability. Even if they do not, however, it is in the American interest to divest itself of that capability so that the Soviets, in a crisis, are not tempted to fire for fear of losing much of their capability to attack.

It is sometimes suggested that this strategy would necessarily mean that American strategic forces would be targeted solely or primarily on cities. This is not so. The United States could maintain the capability to attack a range of targets including theater forces, industrial capacity, and even missile silos. All that would be eschewed is the ability to attack all or most of the Soviet strategic forces quickly.

The best example of a weapons system that does not threaten the Soviet ICBM force is a missile not sufficiently accurate to destroy Soviet missile silos. For many years SLBMs were such weapons—effective threats against targets such as cities but not against protected silos. Unfortunately, American missiles have now advanced beyond their former limits on precision, and the D–5 missile now being developed for the Trident submarines will be accurate enough to threaten Soviet missile silos.

Given such improvements in weapons design, limiting the threat to Soviet strategic forces must be achieved in other ways: (1) by reducing the explosive power of American warheads, (2) by slowing an American attack, or (3) by reducing the ability to launch a strategic attack on the Soviets by surprise. The latter two options are, of course, exactly the *opposite* of the current requirements to be able to fire quickly and without warning.

With regard to the first option, the United States could, for example, replace the multiple warheads in the Minuteman silos not with the larger and more destructive MX missile but with the so-called Midgetman. The single warhead on this missile could be designed to be too small to pose a serious threat to hardened Soviet missile silos.

The second and third options could take a number of dramatic forms. The United States could, for example, place its fixed land-based missiles in deep underground silos and design them to fire only after being popped up to the surface. A mechanism readily visible to Soviet technical means of detection, could be installed to raise the missiles over several hours' time. The United States could even invite the Soviets to station on-site monitors to confirm that the missiles were not being raised.

The military could deploy a significant portion of its force in cruise missiles, which fly much more slowly than ballistic missiles, aboard bombers or submarines. This would make it much harder for the United States to coordinate an attack, but would still give the Soviets little warning time since cruise missiles are very difficult to detect. The United States could deploy its ballistic-carrying submarines in waters too distant from the Soviet Union to target protected silos accurately.

The United States could also take several measures to assure the Soviets that it could not launch a surprise attack to destroy their command and control systems and render a retaliatory strike impossible. First, the United States could withdraw those missiles in Europe that can reach targets in the Soviet Union in only minutes. Second, the United States could refrain from testing SLBMs in low trajectories, which would permit them to arrive on targets very quickly and without warning. And third, the United States could also issue an announcement that it would never attack command and control centers because of its desire to negotiate an end to a nuclear conflict if one were to begin.

The third criterion that should guide the design of the American strategic nuclear posture is that the forces should be able to survive a Soviet attack and remain viable for days while the president or his successor decides what action to take. Most U.S. forces are, in fact, survivable now. The most vulnerable parts of the entire strategic force are the command and control systems. At present, these systems are designed with the assumption that only brief communication with the National Command Authority, as the president and his successors are known, is necessary to receive an order to fire and that the rest of the system need not survive for long.

The United States must develop survivable command centers with redundant capability to communicate with the strategic forces and with the president or his designated representative. It needs to develop means to assess damage after an attack and to make that information available to decision-makers. The essential point is that survivability of communications is not now a high priority it needs to be.

If it did become a high priority, many steps could be taken to ensure that the ability to control the strategic forces would exist for several days after a Soviet attack. At the same time, the United States must establish plans for communicating with the Kremlin in order to negotiate an end to a strategic nuclear exchange. Otherwise, plans to maintain control over nuclear forces several days into a potential conflict may, from a Soviet perspective, look like plans to fight and survive such a war. Changes in American command and control should be fully explained to both the American and the Soviet public.

The three criteria I have laid out here are in no way incompatible with each other. Taken together, they suggest a force consisting of small, single-warhead ballistic missiles deployed in deep underground silos and in both deep- and shallow-water small submarines. This force would be complemented by cruise missiles deployed on bombers, which cannot penetrate Soviet air space quickly, and on submarines.

As Richard Garwin, who advocates a similar posture and from whom many of the ideas presented here are taken, points out, the United States can deploy this posture in the absence of an agreement, and it is in its interest to do so regardless of how or whether the Soviets respond.[6] However, it would be far preferable to move toward such a posture in the context of an arms control agreement with the Soviet Union that first freezes strategic forces and then seeks reductions, thereby securing the objectives of this posture without spending vast sums for new strategic forces. This is true as well for the other proposed changes in the U.S. nuclear posture.

Separating Nuclear and Conventional Forces

The second major change that needs to be made is to separate American nuclear forces from the rest of the military forces, except for the NATO nuclear command. In order for this change to be effective, the remaining military forces, as I will describe in the two following chapters, would have to be made nonnuclear in every respect. Once that is done, the procedures for alerting the conventional forces should be divorced from those alerting the strategic forces. (The NATO nuclear force would have to be related to both the European conventional forces and the strategic nuclear forces, for reasons I will explain in the next chapter.) The president should be able to order an alert that begins to mobilize some or all of the conventional forces without automatically placing the strategic nuclear forces or the NATO nuclear forces on alert. He should also have the capability to order the strategic nuclear forces into alert status, which improves their survivability but not their capacity to fire quickly, without simultaneously alerting the conventional forces.

It would also be necessary to reorganize the strategic nuclear force structure into a single command and perhaps even into a new and separate military service. The least sweeping change would simply direct the navy to group its strategic nuclear delivery systems into a separate nuclear command and to leave the coordination of SAC and the navy nuclear command to the kind of joint planning the SIOP induces. The next step would be to assign all the navy strategic forces—the various submarines deploying ballistic and cruise missiles—to SAC, which would then become, in the jargon of the Pentagon, a "unified" rather than a "specified" command. That is, the SAC commander would have under him both the air force and navy strategic forces.

This is not as radical a proposal as it may seem. Oddly, SAC is now the only command that includes solely the forces of one military service. The command structure was created precisely to bring the forces deployed for a single purpose under a single military officer, no matter what service they belong to. At a minimum, the United States needs a strategic commander who understands that his function is to develop procedures for using nuclear devices at the direction of the president and not to be ready to fight a military campaign or to support ongoing military operations. This command structure should have its own communications and intelligence systems dedicated to detecting and assessing any

Soviet military attack on the United States and responding to it when ordered to do so.

There is a strong case for going one major step further and creating a separate military service for the strategic nuclear forces, as the Soviets have done. One purpose of this move would be to emphasize the distinction between the military services' role, which would be to fight conventional wars, and the role of the strategic service, which would be to maintain nuclear forces for use only at the specific direction of and in a manner ordered by the president.

Unless a separate new service is created, the strategic nuclear posture, regardless of presidential orders, would be constrained by the organizational interests of the existing military services, by their standard operating procedures, and by the agreements that assign particular forces to specific services.

Let me give one example. Richard Garwin, among others, has proposed that the United States deploy a new ICBM in small submarines that would operate just off the coast of the United States. A prestigious panel assembled by the congressional Office of Technology Assessment concluded this option had many advantages. It would, for example, permit the mobility necessary to prevent easy Soviet targeting and yet by-pass the communications problems of deep-water submarines. Even though the Pentagon has been unable to find a suitable basing mode for the new ICBM, it has never taken this option seriously. The reason is that, under the Key West Agreement, any sea-based system would belong to the navy. The air force is not willing to give up the ICBM force, and the navy is not interested in acquiring it. Even the creation of a joint strategic command would not change this situation. The navy would still be responsible for developing the system, and its cost would be part of the navy budget.

If the development and the funding for strategic forces, along with deployment, are left to the existing military services, they will continue to reflect the services' interests, priorities, and standard procedures. The air force will continue to emphasize airplanes over missiles. The navy will continue to perform what it views as the national service of providing one leg of the nuclear defense triad but would resist doing more; it also would fight the incorporation of its submarines into a strategic command. Neither service would devote the substantial resources necessary to ensure the survival of the strategic systems and their communication links with the president.

More generally, the existing services would continue to view the nuclear forces as weapons systems and develop plans to use them in military operations. They would resist what they would view as dangerous and inappropriate meddling by civilians in preparations for war, fearing that any such procedures would set a dangerous precedent for conventional military operations.

A new service would have a number of advantages. Perhaps most important, its very existence would underscore the fact that the traditional military services were in the business of fighting conventional wars, and only conventional wars. To emphasize this, the new service should be given responsibility for providing the nuclear forces for the European theater. In addition, the new service would be created with a different rationale and method of operation. Its nucleus should be those on the missile command side of SAC and the air force. The service would have authority to develop, operate, and control any system for the delivery of nuclear weapons, no matter where it was deployed. It would create standard operating procedures based on the understanding of what its purpose is and under what circumstances it would be used. Civilian officials could determine its overall budget and influence its internal priorities more than they do with the existing services. The strategic service would also take over responsibility from the Department of Energy for the production of nuclear devices. It might report to the secretary of defense and the president through a separate channel under the chairman of the Joint Chiefs of Staff.

Crisis Policy

Perhaps the most important dimension of an alternative strategic nuclear posture is the development of new operating rules for behavior in a crisis. As I have stated earlier, under the plans now in effect, U.S. nuclear forces move with the rest of the forces closer to firing as the alert status increases. The new posture, recommended earlier by McGeorge Bundy as well as by Bruce Blair, would direct the American strategic forces to ride out and survive a Soviet attack rather than to plan on firing as soon after a Soviet launch as possible. Blair, who labels this policy "no immediate second use," presents an authoritative and succinct explanation of how it would work in practice.

> The response to impending or actual Soviet nuclear attack would initially be geared to ensuring the survival of the forces and command structures. Under current arrangements, protective dispersal and other survival actions are related organically to preparations for immediate retaliation. Under a doctrine of no immediate second use, survival actions would be separate from and would take strong precedence over counterattack coordination during and after a Soviet first strike. Authority to conduct offensive operations would be withheld for at least twenty-four hours, and military units would be programmed to operate accordingly.
>
> Because retaliation would be eliminated as an organizational priority during an attack, the main purpose of early warning systems would be to alert units to an impending strike and trigger preprogrammed responses that would minimize their exposure. Because early warning systems would not be required to support an early decision to retaliate, the United States could design them to meet the narrower requirements of organizational survival. Planned improvements in early warning sensors, computers, communications and so forth would be judged solely on the basis of their potential contribution to this objective.[7]

As Blair goes on to point out, this posture would require tightening of negative controls by putting locks on all the weapons and by removing any pre-delegated authority to release strategic nuclear devices. At the same time, he notes, authority to take steps to ensure survival could be delegated to all units.

> Activities associated with force and command survival could be highly decentralized. Because these activities would be purely defensive, nuclear units at all levels, including the lowest echelon, could be pro-

grammed for rapid dispersion and could be granted unprecedented authority to take whatever unplanned steps would be necessary for their continuing survival. Various information channels, particularly tactical warning circuits, would have to be modified to provide maximum support for this decentralized activity. Direct links between warning sensors and individual units, for instance, could be installed.[8]

Blair then explains how the adoption of this posture would affect the operations of the strategic bomber fleet.

Among the three force components, bombers would be most affected by this reposturing. Under current arrangements, alert bombers with traditional SIOP missions launch on tactical warning and fly toward loiter orbits on the periphery of enemy territory in anticipation of the imminent dissemination of retaliatory orders. Under the proposed doctrine, bombers would launch on tactical warning, but they would not leave the continental United States until retaliation had been authorized: they would thus operate like strategic reserve bombers. Bomber takeoff, flight profiles, tanker rendezvous, and recovery would have to be designed to ensure the continuing survival and coherence of the force and could not be offensive.[9]

Because this new posture is so radically different from that which currently guides the strategic nuclear posture, its implementation would require an explicit presidential directive indicating that the strategic nuclear forces will under no circumstances fire first. The directive would also need to spell out very clearly the doctrine of no early second use as well as the design characteristics of the force described above and changes in command arrangements. The additional step of the creation of a new service would require legislation.

DIPLOMATIC AND MILITARY CONSEQUENCES OF THE NEW POSTURE

It is difficult to find anyone who believes that the United States should threaten or contemplate launching a strategic first blow, except in response to a Soviet attack in Europe or unmistakable signs that the Soviets are launching an attack on the United States. Thus, the objections to adopting a new policy would appear to be limited to these two:

1. It would reduce the credibility of the American nuclear deterrent in Europe.

2. It would permit Soviet blackmail in a crisis because the Soviets could threaten to strike first and gain an advantage with no fear of an American preemptive first strike in response to such a threat.

It is true that many Europeans now believe that their security depends on the Soviet fear that if war starts in Europe, the United States might fire its strategic forces against the Soviet Union even if the Soviets never launch an attack on the United States. Few believe that the American threat to initiate a strategic exchange deliberately is credible, given the Soviets' unquestioned ability to destroy the United States in retaliation. Thus, insofar as the threat retains some credibility, it is through the mechanism that Thomas Schelling labeled "the threat that leaves something to chance."[10] War, in this view, is deterred precisely by the system's potential to get out of control and explode. American security rests on a doomsday machine linked to a roulette wheel.

There is no doubt that this aspect of deterrence would be reduced by adopting the strategic nuclear posture proposed here. But there are several compelling arguments for proceeding with it nonetheless.

- First, as I will discuss in detail in the next chapter, there is every reason to believe that other factors, including fear of conventional war and the fact that events in Western Europe do not threaten Soviet interests, are sufficient to deter a Soviet attack. These factors also prevent the Soviets from credibly threatening to use force.

- Second, it is simply unacceptable, given that the survival of the planet is at risk, to rely on a doomsday machine linked to a roulette wheel to defend American interests.

- Third, no matter what steps the United States takes, there will remain some risk that it will stumble into nuclear war with the Soviet Union. This unalterable possibility will induce Soviet caution even if the United States redesigns its strategic posture so as to reduce the risk of accidental nuclear war.

- Fourth, equally important to Soviet leaders is the possibility that the United States would retain the ability—however delayed and selective—to fire first with nuclear weapons.

- Finally, if the United States concludes that, with the reduced risk of an accidental nuclear war, the deterrent in Europe is not satisfactory, it should and could take other steps to reduce the risk of war or Soviet blackmail.

In the next chapter I will outline how the ideas presented in this chapter could be implemented in Europe without incurring any significant cost. Certainly no European government, including West Germany, could object to measures that were publicly described as steps designed to prevent accidental war.

All of these points apply as well to the effect of the proposed changes on crisis threats arising in areas outside of Europe. Given the retaliatory capability that each side now has, it is difficult to see how the Soviets could make a credible threat even if they could destroy much of the American land-based missile force in a first strike. It is also difficult to believe, as I have argued, that the American threat to strike first is an effective means of coercion.

By lessening the U.S. capability of destroying a major portion of Soviet forces on first strike, the strategic nuclear policy I propose would reduce the Soviets' incentive to strike first, either to secure an advantage or to preempt a feared American attack. The new posture would further diminish the credibility of a Soviet threat to strike first by dismantling the targets they might attack successfully and by strengthening the American ability to survive a Soviet attack with forces and command and control systems in place. In addition, it would reduce the possibility that nuclear devices would be fired accidentally or inadvertently, a likelihood that is, in my view, far greater than the deliberate initiation of nuclear war.

Just as significantly, this proposed nuclear posture would give the president more time to respond to a Soviet attack and would reduce the danger of placing him in a "use-them-or-lose-them" situation where he feels he must retaliate quickly or lose the power to retaliate at all. The critical factor limiting the quality of information provided to the president and his response time is the survivability of command and control systems. To the extent that such capabilities can be enhanced, the president's ability to react responsibly will be improved. Thus the president would have time to learn the nature of the attack on the United States—who perpetrated it, what targets have been destroyed, and what is the objective of the attack—and to consult with his advisers. He could then decide whether to order an attack and, if so, to determine against what targets.

The proposed posture would in no way limit the president's options in responding to a nuclear attack on the United States. It is true that U.S. forces would not be able to attack Soviet missiles, which will already have been fired, or Soviet command systems. But this does not leave Soviet cities as the only possible targets. The president could order attacks on Soviet industrial targets, such as oil fields, or on Soviet general force deployments. The strategic force planners would be instructed to develop a range of options, including strikes on cities.

Perhaps most important, this proposed nuclear posture would give greater flexibility to a resolute and responsible president in an international crisis before the situation degenerates into a nuclear attack. Today a president, confronted with world events that seem to call at the very least for the alerting of U.S. military forces and perhaps for their use, faces a terrible dilemma: He can choose not to move the force to an alert status, a decision that could jeopardize American interests, or he can alert forces, which means also alerting the nuclear forces and beginning to remove the controls on their use, thereby increasing the risk of detonation.

U.S. military policy need not force a president to this choice. It should allow him to bring the conventional military power of the United States to bear on a crisis without inevitably increasing the risk of nuclear war very substantially. Of course, any use of American power, or threat of its use, carries with it the danger of an explosion to nuclear war, but American policy should seek to reduce those risks to the degree possible. It must help to avoid not only stumbling into nuclear war but also tying the hands of a president who suddenly discovers in the midst of a crisis just how dangerous all his choices are.

5 NUCLEAR STRATEGY IN EUROPE

From the beginning, American nuclear policy has concentrated on protecting Europe from a Soviet invasion. For forty years, U.S. nuclear posture has assumed that NATO forces could not win a conventional war in Europe and that a conventional Soviet attack might have to be countered with a nuclear response.

As a result, nowhere in the world is the legacy of the Eisenhower directives on nuclear policy stronger than in Europe. Today, though official NATO doctrine calls for the treatment of nuclear devices as special weapons, much of the force posture, planning, and attitudes of the military and civilian leadership in Europe reveals the underlying strength of the idea that nuclear devices are regular weapons. More than 5,000 American nuclear devices are stored on the European continent, and thousands more at sea are earmarked for use in the European theater.

Furthermore, as I stated in the last chapter, though antinuclear sentiment runs high among the European population, some Europeans (including some political leaders) regard the nuclear devices there as a kind of "security blanket." They believe their safety depends on the Soviet belief that an invasion of Western Europe would automatically lead to a nuclear attack on the Soviet homeland.

As with strategic weapons, I am convinced that it is possible to alter nuclear policy in Europe so that NATO security is less dependent on this nuclear threat. However, given the strong legacy of the Eisenhower directives and the widespread reliance on nuclear devices as a security blanket, implementing a new nuclear posture will be more difficult in Europe than anywhere else in the world.

THE CURRENT NUCLEAR POSTURE

The roots of today's NATO nuclear posture were seeded during the Eisenhower administration. Nuclear devices were turned over to the military services, which were authorized to plan for their use in any conflict and to deploy them with American forces wherever they were stationed, subject only to the approval of the host country. The State Department was authorized to seek approval for the deployment of nuclear devices in every NATO country and to offer each nation an agreement to train and equip their armed forces to fight with nuclear devices. Warheads for use by these other nations would be stored in Europe and made available when the Alliance decided to employ nuclear weapons.

In the early 1960s, the Kennedy administration began pressing for a change in NATO strategy, that would reduce its reliance on nuclear devices and lead to an improvement in the conventional capability of the Alliance. These proposals were ultimately incorporated into the official NATO strategy in 1968. Today, NATO strategy provides that a conventional attack should be met by conventional means to the degree possible.

Advocates of this new strategy within the Kennedy administration hoped and expected that it would lead to changes in war plans, procurement programs, and deployment policies. However, NATO strategy continued to assert that nuclear weapons would be used when and if "necessary." As a result, the change in official strategy has had little effect on the nature of the nuclear posture of the Alliance. In order to implement this doctrine of flexible response, the NATO military commanders must be ready to use nuclear weapons at any time, and especially when they are conducting conventional military operations. Thus, American forces in Europe, and those of European allies who are willing to participate, are still ready at any moment to initiate the use of nuclear devices. The nuclear posture is designed for the rapid and widespread first use of nuclear weapons. Despite the policy changes, there have been no fundamental changes in NATO nuclear procedures since the early 1950s.

The same is true of deployment. The size and composition of the NATO nuclear force have varied only slightly since the end of the Eisenhower administration. Seven NATO allies— Belgium, Germany, Great Britain, Greece, Italy, the Netherlands, and Turkey—permit nuclear weapons to be stored on their territory, and all have dual-capable weapons systems that would be matched up with American nuclear devices in the event of an Alliance decision to prepare for nuclear war. In 1985 airplane bombs and artillery shells each made up approximately one-third of the 5,000 nuclear devices that were stored in Europe. The other third ran the gamut from the new long-range cruise and Pershing missiles to so-called atomic demolition munitions, or ADMs, which are small weapons that would be planted in the ground and blown up.

The weapons range in yield from fractions of a kiloton to megatons for aircraft bombs. Some weapons have variable yields, any one of which can be selected depending on the target. Although they are described as battlefield weapons, most are as large as or larger than the Hiroshima and Nagasaki bombs. Most of the nuclear delivery systems are dual capable.

An overwhelming majority of the NATO nuclear warheads are located in West Germany. In their book *Nuclear Battlefields*, written in 1984, William Arkin and Richard Fieldhouse report that 3,400 warheads, under the control of six foreign nations, are scattered in dozens of sites throughout the country from the Danish border on the north to the Swiss border on the south. Furthermore:

> There are more short-range nuclear artillery weapons in West Germany than any other nuclear weapon (over 100 nuclear-capable artillery units and 1,500 warheads). Second in number are surface-to-surface missiles such as Lance and Pershing. There are 78 NATO

Lance launchers and 600 warheads in Germany, 126 Pershing 1a launchers (72 West German and 54 U.S.), and 54 U.S. Pershing IIs. . . . Five types of aircraft at eight bases in West Germany also have nuclear missions. These include U.S. and West German units (with U.S. nuclear warheads) and British units. There are approximately 500 nuclear bombs for these aircraft. Other nuclear systems include Nike-Hercules surface-to-air missiles, with some 300 nuclear warheads, and about 250 atomic demolition munitions (ADMs).[1]

Remarkably, no centralized organization controls all of NATO's theater nuclear forces. Outside of Germany, NATO's nuclear posture is decentralized and dispersed. Though the other six NATO countries hosting U.S. nuclear devices have bombs for fighter-bombers and nuclear artillery, no other European county has every type of nuclear weapons. Other nuclear systems are also widely dispersed.[2]

This dispersed posture has led NATO to create a sprawling, decentralized system that gives rise to serious problems for the Alliance. As Paul Bracken wrote in his 1983 book, *The Command and Control of Nuclear Forces*, this lack of centralized organization, while noticeable in strategic forces to some degree, is particularly troublesome in theater forces, which are dispersed over many different commands and subcommands. Bracken explains it this way:

> Nuclear artillery, battlefield support missiles, and naval weapons are all controlled by different organizations. It is not so much the large variety of theater nuclear weapons that is important as it is the large number of different organizations and lines of authority that have responsibility for determining how these weapons are used. Army divisions, aircraft carrier groups, fighter squadrons, commando teams, and air defense units all have their own nuclear weapons. The coordination necessary for a centrally directed, and politically controlled, conflict is made difficult by the large number of different organizations whose actions must be coordinated. Moreover, each of these organizations is designed and trained to complete its own peculiar mission. The training, indoctrination, and "corporate culture" of each of them will powerfully affect their actions in time of war.[3]

Most of the warheads in Europe are stored in specially designed nuclear storage sites in the six countries that permit nuclear warheads on their territory. These storage sites are uniquely marked, and their locations are well known to the Soviet military. If war broke out in Europe, the storage sites would be very vulnerable to attack by conventional as well as nuclear means.

Some nuclear weapons are already dispersed to American units that are on alert. The quick reaction alert (QRA) forces include the cruise and Pershing missiles and various bomber aircraft, such as the F-111 and the F-4. These systems are ready to deliver nuclear weapons, and most can reach targets in the Soviet Union as well as those on the European battlefield. Other nuclear weapons stored in Europe away from combat units would be dispersed in wartime to different commanders.[4]

In addition to the American nuclear devices in Europe, the British and the French have their own nuclear forces. On the other side of the line, the Soviet Union has an array of nuclear-capable forces and, at least since 1984, has stored nuclear weapons in Eastern Europe.

NATO has never faced a crisis in which it came close to going to war or to using nuclear devices. It is difficult to predict what would actually happen if the United States and West Germany considered the prospect of using military force. NATO plans call for consultation both about the decision to go to war and about the decision to use nuclear devices.

Under existing plans, if NATO forces began to fight, NATO commanders would initiate preparations for the use of nuclear devices. They would begin to move the nuclear warheads out of the nuclear storage sites to prevent their destruction and to reduce the time necessary to start using them. NATO military commanders would begin conducting conventional military operations, but with the knowledge that they might, at any time, be directed to initiate the use of nuclear devices. Military commanders are likely to withhold dual-capable aircraft and missiles to keep them ready to deliver nuclear devices. Once they authorized conventional military operations, the NATO countries would begin consultation about whether and how to use nuclear devices.[5]

For more than twenty years, NATO defense ministers meeting in the NATO Nuclear Planning Group have attempted to develop plans for the use of nuclear devices in Europe. They have agreed that the first use of such devices should be a demonstration shot designed to indicate to the Kremlin that the war is getting out of hand. There is no agreement beyond that. Not only has the Nuclear Planning Group failed to reach a consensus, but no one has even been able to put forward a persuasive plan for using nuclear weapons on the central front in Europe.[6]

NATO strategy calls for an escalation to nuclear warfare only if a conventional attack cannot be repelled by conventional means. But because of the reluctance of some commanders to use dual-capable forces early in a conventional war, and because of the need to consult with Alliance members on the use of nuclear devices, the Alliance probably would be forced to decide whether to use nuclear weapons long before NATO's conventional defense has been fully tested. If a Soviet conventional attack appeared to be succeeding, NATO might introduce short-range nuclear artillery or long-range theater weapons to attack assets in the enemy rear, such as second-echelon forces. If their use did not turn the tide, strategic nuclear weapons targeted on the Soviet Union would be launched.

In short, more than thirty years after nuclear devices were first deployed in Europe, it remains true that NATO does not know how to

- win a war using nuclear devices,
- continue to fight a war on the battlefield once nuclear bombs are used,
- avoid destroying the country it is seeking to defend once nuclear devices are used, or
- stop a nuclear war once it has started.

Despite efforts to the contrary, NATO strategy continues to rest not on the ability to defeat the enemy on the battlefield but on the threat of first use of theater and, ultimately, strategic nuclear forces. In other words, as I suggested in the previous chapter, NATO's defense of Europe consists of a doomsday machine linked to a roulette wheel.

THE PROPOSED NUCLEAR POSTURE

As with strategic weapons, an alternative nuclear posture for Europe logically emerges if one treats nuclear explosives as devices rather than as weapons. Before I begin to sketch out this proposal, however, let me state that what I am suggesting is not, strictly speaking, a no-first-use policy for Europe. It is a somewhat different proposal—one that focuses not on a public promise never to use nuclear weapons first, but rather on the forces and operational plans for nuclear and conventional weapons in Europe.

If nuclear devices were not treated as weapons, NATO's conventional military forces would be completely separated from the specialized units designed to deliver nuclear explosive devices should the political leadership of the Alliance ever decide to employ them.

All so-called dual-capable systems would be eliminated. The military forces of the Alliance, including the American forces, would be equipped and trained as if nuclear explosive devices did not exist; their mission would be to fight and win conventional wars. An entirely separate structure would be assigned the task of delivering nuclear devices. This force might be placed directly under the supreme allied commander in Europe (SACEUR), the American general in charge of NATO military operations. SACEUR now directly controls the ground-launched cruise missiles and Pershing II missiles recently deployed in Europe. The NATO nuclear force would, however, be totally divorced from the command structure for conducting conventional combat operations. It would have a separate command and control structure and would not be deployed at regular military bases.

The special nuclear strike force could be deployed somewhere in the European theater. Since it should be invulnerable to an attack and not in danger of being overrun, there is a strong argument for putting it at sea under NATO's command or for relying on U.S. strategic submarines. However, other basing modes are conceivable, including the helicopter-deployed force that William Kaufmann has suggested.[7] Alternatively, the warheads could be attached to air-launched cruise missiles deployed on bombers that are based in the United States but ready to fly to Europe. In any event, the NATO nuclear force would have to be capable of surviving a conventional war in Europe as well as a Soviet effort to destroy it with either conventional or nuclear explosives.

Since the nuclear forces would not be highly vulnerable to attack, and since their task would not be to fight a war, the number of nuclear devices needed would be substantially fewer than the seven to eight thousand now deployed in Europe and nearby at sea. In all probability, several hundred would be more than enough. The most likely targets for such a force would be Warsaw Pact reserve units and air bases.

The nuclear force would retain the capability to be used first, and it could be employed at the direction of the president of the United States in consultation with other NATO allies. However, NATO would no longer threaten first use, and military planning would be based on the assumption that NATO would not initiate the use of nuclear weapons. In the event of conventional hostilities, NATO's regular military forces would be able to go on alert without increasing the risk of unauthorized use of nuclear weapons, without holding weapons systems in reserve for the delivery of nuclear explosive devices, and without allocating forces to protect these systems. Whether or not NATO spent more money on conventional forces or changed the nature of its conventional deployments, it would have to rely more on conventional force to deter or respond to Soviet actions in Europe.

ADVANTAGES AND DISADVANTAGES

Assessing the costs and gains of such a posture involves answering two critical and related questions. First, How would the proposed changes in the NATO nuclear posture affect the deterrence of Soviet moves in Europe to which the

West would object? And second, How would the changes affect the probability of nuclear war?

The major objection raised against all proposals to reduce NATO's reliance on nuclear explosive devices is that they would substantially increase the risk of war—nuclear and conventional. This perspective is based, for the most part, on three assumptions: (1) the Soviet Union has strong political incentives to invade Western Europe; (2) the Kremlin has confidence in its ability to win a quick conventional victory; and (3) the NATO threat to use nuclear explosive devices is credible to the Soviet Union and has an important effect on its actions.

These assumptions have generally been accepted by those who have debated issues of NATO strategy and nuclear war. I believe all three are false. In my view, adoption of the recommended package would not increase the likelihood of a Soviet attack and might actually discourage it further by increasing the credibility of NATO's threat to fight an extended conventional war. Let me examine each of these three assumptions in detail.

Political Incentives

It is certainly true that the Kremlin sometimes uses force as an instrument of policy. But that does not mean that if it could be confident of victory, the leadership of the Soviet Union would necessarily launch a military attack in Europe or use the credible threat of such an attack to secure a diplomatic advantage. There have been instances when the Soviet Union possessed the military capability to employ force effectively but chose not to do so. The overriding reason has not been the military situation; rather, in those cases, the Soviets have lacked a strong political incentive to justify such military risks.

Generally, the most critical variable has been whether there is something already happening across the border that poses a serious danger to Soviet interests as they are defined in the Kremlin. The Soviet invasions of Czechoslovakia and

Hungary clearly fit this pattern. When the Soviets moved, it was not because the military balance had shifted in its favor but because the cost of not using military force had substantially increased.

This does not mean that NATO countries must avoid taking actions that they would otherwise take for fear of provoking a Soviet attack. It means only that the actions that America's allies take in their own interests do not threaten Soviet interests and are not likely to do so in the future. Indeed, they have not done so for the past forty years.

The primary Soviet objective in Western Europe is to prevent the reemergence of a German state with the independence and military power to pose a threat to Soviet interests. The striking fact is that NATO and its members, including West Germany, share this objective. That is why West Germany has renounced the development of an independent German army and nuclear capability: in order to assure the German people, Germany's allies, and the Soviet Union that Germany would not again pose a threat to European security.

Thus, the dominant objectives of NATO and its allies in Europe should be to maintain a political situation in Germany that permits the perpetuation of free democratic institutions without posing a threat to the Soviet Union. In order to accomplish this objective, the West must continue to persuade Germany that the Alliance will deter Soviet attacks effectively, so that Germany has nothing to fear from the Soviets. Furthermore, it needs to accomplish this goal in a way that does not run a high risk of nuclear war and that, in fact, does deter Soviet attacks.

This factor is far more critical than any shifts in the NATO nuclear posture or the conventional military balance. If the Alliance fails in its role of convincing Germany that it is protected, if West Germany decides that it needs to rearm and acquire nuclear weapons, or if the Soviets decide that developments in West Germany are a threat to its vital interests, then the danger of war would increase dramatically. The danger of war would also significantly increase if other events occurred that affected Soviet or German interests, such as a workers' uprising in East Germany that Soviet troops were called in to suppress or a revolt in an East European country. Such spontaneous events cannot, of course, be deterred by changes in the East–West military balance.

The basic point is that nations, including the Soviet Union, do not go to war simply because they believe that the military balance is in their favor. They go to war, even if they perceive the balance as unfavorable, if they see no acceptable alternative. If NATO is successful at preserving the current situation in West Germany and at negotiating solutions to other problems as they arise, the details of the military balance will be less important.

The Possibility of a Quick Soviet Victory

The military balance is not irrelevant, however. If the temptation is great enough, a nation may attack or threaten the use of military force to improve its situation. It would be foolhardy in the extreme to present the Kremlin with a military vacuum in the center of Europe. Many descriptions of the NATO–Warsaw Pact conventional military balance suggest that the absence of nuclear weapons and credible nuclear threats would create such a vacuum. The Soviets, believing themselves capable of securing a quick military victory on the central front, might move to exploit this advantage. This is often cited as the decisive objection to reducing reliance on the threat of first use.

Put in its starkest form, the argument is that if the Kremlin came to believe that there were no chance that NATO would initiate the use of nuclear devices, it would order an attack, knowing that Soviet troops could easily defeat the NATO military forces in a conventional war. Leaving aside for a moment the question of whether NATO declaration could assure the Soviet leadership that nuclear devices would never be used, I want to explore briefly the nature of the conventional balance.

NATO military commanders have never been willing to assure the political leaders of the Alliance that they could successfully defend Europe in a conventional war. This should not be surprising. Military leaders always want larger forces. In addition, because of the emphasis that NATO puts on nuclear operations, the capacity of existing forces for sustained conventional operations is not as large as it could be.

Moreover, there is no scientific way to determine the outcome of a conventional war between two opposing forces. An enormous number of uncertainties affect the outcome. Thus it is not surprising that the NATO military commanders, who would be responsible in wartime, are very cautious. However, we can expect Soviet military planners also to be cautious. Soviet political leaders are well aware of the uncertainties at home and, having lived through a conventional war, are unlikely to view it as an acceptable alternative.

Indeed, there is every reason to believe that the Soviet leaders are very uncertain about the outcome of conventional war between NATO and the Warsaw Pact. Just as NATO military commanders point with concern to those categories in which the Soviets have an advantage—the number of divisions and tanks, surprise, unity of command, and so forth—so Soviet military planners must highlight such NATO advantages as superiority of weapons systems, the unreliability of Warsaw Pact troops from countries other than the Soviet Union, the danger of sabotage of supply lines, and the need to maintain forces at the Chinese front.

Calculations about the likely outcome of a war are also critically dependent on how much warning time each side has and what each does with that time. For example, would the United States mobilize and start sending troops to Europe if tensions increased greatly? Victory in a conventional war also turns on the morale and loyalty of the troops, the skill of the generals, and the willingness of the populaton to support a long war if necessary. Judgments about these issues are exceedingly hard to make in peacetime. All reduce Soviet confidence in success on the battlefield.

The Politburo is acutely aware of the possible domestic consequences in the Soviet Union and Eastern Europe of a protracted conventional war. It knows from Russian history that domestic upheavals, including revolutions, have often been stimulated by foreign wars. Thus, war in Europe may quickly lead to convulsions among the peoples of Eastern Europe even if the Soviet Union is successful on the battlefield. To attack Western Europe, the Soviet Union must be confident not only of a victory but of a quick victory.

In considering the military aspects of a decision to start a war, the Politburo must ask itself two key questions: (1) Will NATO resist? and (2) What weapons will it use in the resistance? Those in the West who fear a reduced reliance on nuclear devices consider the second question the more important one and that if the answer to the second precludes nuclear first use, the Soviets will be ready to attack.

I believe that the answer to the first question is far more important. The Soviet leadership is anxious to avoid a war with the United States and hence would focus much more on the West's willingness to fight than on what weapons it would use. As noted above, the Kremlin is by no means confident of quick victory in a conventional war or ready to fight such a war. Soviet leaders must believe that, once a war begins, the United States would fight as long as necessary to win and would mobilize the necessary domestic resources. Moreover, nothing calls into question NATO's resolve to fight more than its need to decide quickly whether to introduce nuclear devices.

The Credibility of a NATO Nuclear Threat

In exploring the question of deterrence, one central question needs to be asked: Are there any circumstances in which the Soviets would attack if they believed that NATO would resist only with conventional weapons, but would not attack if they concluded that NATO intended to use nuclear devices? I believe the answer to this question is no.

As I stated before, one important reason is the Soviets' desire to avoid a conventional war. Another is the uncertainty about whether the war would actually end without the use of nuclear devices. Critics of any possible changes in the NATO posture often assume that, in the current situation, the Russians are sure that NATO would use nuclear devices and that, following any changes in the posture, they would be equally sure that NATO would not use nuclear devices. In fact, as the Soviets are well aware, nothing in international politics is so certain.

There is some significant possibility now that nuclear devices would be used without a clear decision by the American president. However, it is not certain that the situation would get out of hand, nor is it certain that NATO would make the decision to use nuclear devices if it faced defeat in a conventional war. When the leaders of Germany come face-to-face with the consequences of unleashing nuclear conflict on their own territory, they might well conclude that they should negotiate an end to the conflict without resorting to nuclear warfare. Indeed, if NATO's political leadership believe that they would need to use nuclear devices within a few days (if not a few hours), they might not be able to make the decision to go to war at all,

The Kremlin is well aware of all of this. In planning an attack in the current situation, Soviet leaders would know that the likelihood of a nuclear response was significant, but they would rate the probability as less than certain. By the same token, if NATO were to adopt the posture suggested here, the Soviet leadership still could not rate the probability of a nuclear response as zero or close to it because of what McGeorge Bundy has called "existential deterrence": Regardless of their declaratory and deployment policies, as long as both sides possess nuclear devices there is a probability that nuclear explosions will occur before a war was brought to an end.[8]

Thus, given the confusion and loss of control that develop in the fog of war, the Soviet leaders would know that the use of nuclear devices was possible regardless of the stated intentions or plans of the Alliance. Their calculation of the odds would change depending on the NATO posture, but such calculations would be surrounded by great uncertainty and, therefore, would be unlikely to tilt the balance decisively if an invasion were being considered. In fact, NATO's determination to resist conventionally and, if necessary, over a long period could actually increase the possibility that nuclear devices would be used before a war came to an end.

THE DOOMSDAY MACHINE

There is one way to make the probability of nuclear destruction virtually certain if the Soviets take actions in Europe or elsewhere that incite American disapproval. The United States could construct what Herman Kahn called a "doomsday machine"—a device that would automatically detonate and explode a large number of nuclear devices if the Soviets moved across a designated line.[9] The two major problems with such a device are that it might go off by accident and that the United States might not want to destroy the world once the Soviets, by miscalculation or inadvertence, had crossed the line.

In all too many ways, the current NATO nuclear posture resembles Kahn's doomsday machine. This is one of the great dangers in the current posture and one of the significant advantages of moving to the alternative force posture suggested here.

There are a number of ways in which the current NATO nuclear posture could lead to the unintended use of nuclear devices—what Schelling has described as the "threat that leaves something to chance."[10] These possibilities include Soviet preemption, the use-them-or-lose-them syndrome, unauthorized use by battlefield commanders, and uncontrolled escalation. I will discuss each in turn briefly.[11]

Preemption

The existing NATO nuclear posture appears to be designed to encourage a Soviet preemptive strike with conventional or nuclear weapons. Recall that the nuclear devices are stored in some 50 to 100 sites in Western Europe. These sites are uniquely configured so that the Soviets can have no doubt of their location. Some other nuclear devices are with aircraft and missiles, but they are also in a small number of places and are subject to being destroyed in a surprise attack by Soviet missiles. Once a war began, however, the nuclear devices would be widely dispersed and could not be destroyed easily in a single strike. Thus Soviet military plans reportedly call for a preemptive conventional strike designed to destroy the entire arsenal of nuclear devices in the NATO area at the outset of any military clash, before they can be dispersed. Military planners on both sides must believe that such a strike has a high probability of success.

At the same time, the Soviet leaders know that NATO doctrine calls for the use of nuclear devices as soon as NATO military commanders believe they are losing the war. Soviet military planners must therefore assume that nuclear explosive devices would be used before the war came to an end, increasing the incentive to preempt.

Given the high probability that a war in Europe would sooner or later become nuclear, and given the vulnerability of the NATO nuclear arsenal at the start of the conflict, there is a high probability that the Kremlin would authorize a preemptive strike against NATO nuclear storage sites at the outset of any military conflict. Changes in the NATO nuclear posture and in its doctrine for using nuclear explosive devices would alter these incentives.

The Use-Them-or-Lose-Them Syndrome

NATO military commanders are, of course, aware of the vulnerability of their nuclear forces. Thus, in a crisis they would press for authority to launch their alert nuclear forces at the onset of military operations. Failing that, they would request permission to disperse their nuclear-capable delivery systems and to move the nuclear explosive devices from the nuclear storage sites to the forces that would deliver them. Plans exist for such dispersal, and it would be difficult to countermand such orders since that would leave the nuclear forces and weapons in a very vulnerable position. Yet the dispersal itself could set off nuclear war in Europe.

If it does not, American military commanders will be dispersing nuclear explosive devices to their forces and perhaps also to NATO allies. As the conventional conflict progresses, military units that possess nuclear explosive devices will come under attack and will be in danger of being overrun. There will be great pressure on Western civilian leaders to permit those units to use their nuclear explosive devices in an effort to defend themselves. The alternative would be to accept the defeat of a unit without allowing it to use the most "powerful" weapons at its disposal. There would also be the danger that the nuclear explosive devices would be captured by the Warsaw Pact forces. Decisions would have to be made in minutes or hours at most. It is possible that authority to employ nuclear explosive devices would be granted only because of the use-them-or-lose-them situation.

Unauthorized Use

Most agree that the risk of unauthorized or accidental use of nuclear weapons is very, very low in peacetime. The current command and control system is redundant. The risk of unauthorized use in a wartime situation, however, is much greater. In the midst of a conventional conflict, or with the approach of one, many peacetime precautions and controls would be swept away as hampering and impractical.

One example of such a control is permissive action links, or PALS. PALs are essentially electronic locks matched with a nuclear device. Each weapon requires a distinct code to "unlock" it. According to Paul Bracken, military commanders would exert strong pressure to release those codes and unlock the weapons as soon as they leave the centralized storage sites. In peacetime, the PALs serve as a beneficial safeguard against use by terrorists. During war, however, dispersing nuclear devices throughout Europe without first matching those weapons with their codes would make them essentially useless. "Sending thousands of locked weapons into the fog of war," Bracken argues, "flies in the face of every known military tradition." [12]

Once those nuclear devices were unlocked and dispersed throughout Europe, it would be very difficult to maintain centralized control over them. Although military commanders would not lightly disobey orders, unauthorized use by a military commander whose unit is about to be overrun is a real and serious possibility during any European conflict.

Escalation

The wide dispersal of nuclear explosive devices and the asymmetry in the theater nuclear arsenals of the two sides would generate pressure to escalate to the use of nuclear explosive devices very quickly. Once a single nuclear weapon was used, the pressure to respond and to use additional weapons before they could be destroyed would be great indeed. Military commanders are likely to feel that the prohibition on using nuclear explosive devices was removed once a single nuclear warhead had been exploded; political leaders would come under enormous pressure to authorize military commanders to use the nuclear explosive devices at their disposal according to military judgments. In hours, if not minutes, much of Europe would be destroyed and nuclear devices would have exploded on Soviet territory. It is difficult to see how the exchange could be ended short of both sides firing most of their warheads, including those that the United States labeled "strategic."

REDUCING THE LIKELIHOOD
OF NUCLEAR WAR

Each of these pressures toward initial use or escalation of the use of nuclear devices would be substantially reduced if the alternative posture posed here were adopted. The NATO nuclear forces would not be vulnerable to a Soviet attack, reducing the incentive to preempt. The Soviet military planners would not view nuclear war as inevitable and hence would be less likely to press for a preemptive strike. The nuclear explosive devices would not be with the troops, thus eliminating the use-them-or-lose-them syndrome and greatly reducing the risk of unauthorized use. If a single device were used, either inadvertently or by design, there would be less likelihood of sudden escalation.

From one perspective, all of these changes are undesirable. One of the elements that deters war in Europe is "the threat that leaves something to chance." Both sides know that if they initiate military conflict in Europe, it could turn into a nuclear holocaust without anyone intending such an eventuality. The alternative posture would sharply reduce, though it would not eliminate, those risks. In that sense, it might well increase the likelihood of war.

Given its current posture, NATO political leaders would know that if they decided to initiate the use of force, they would very quickly be faced with the need to authorize the use of nuclear weapons or call a halt to the fighting. Given those choices, they might well decide that they could not use military force. If, on the other hand, the posture proposed here were in place, then NATO political leaders would be in a position to consider initiating conventional operations. They would have no greater assurance of victory, but they would know that they would not be confronted almost immediately by a demand from the military commanders to permit first the dispersal and then the use of nuclear weapons.

I believe that the increased possibility of conventional war that may come from adopting this posture is a price worth paying. Whether it is called a doomsday machine or a threat that leaves something to chance, the policy of resting the security of Europe on deliberately creating a situation in which the world would be destroyed if a war begins is irresponsible. And whatever the United States and its allies do, there will be some residual danger that any conflict in Europe would not end short of a strategic nuclear exchange. The West cannot avoid this form of existential deterrence, but it should not exacerbate it or rely on it.

Moreover, as I argued above, the threat of nuclear war is not the only factor that prevents a Soviet attack. Nor is it even the most important. Thus, if NATO fears a war, it is not inevitable that it must fight a war; it can initiate diplomatic negotiations to arrive at solutions that ease the conflict. It can also consider improving its capability to fight a conventional war, but such an increase is not necessary and certainly should not be a precondition for adopting the proposed posture.

If the assertion is made that a reduction in NATO's nuclear force requires an increase in conventional capability, that assertion implies that tactical nuclear weapons can somehow compensate for conventional inferiority. As I demonstrated above, this is simply not true because of all the factors that go into a nation's decision to fight, with or without nuclear devices. If NATO's conventional forces would be insufficient after the Alliance changes its nuclear posture, then the conventional forces are insufficient now. NATO needs to decide what fighting capability it needs. To the degree that it wants to attain that capability, it must develop conventional forces; there is no way to fight with nuclear explosive devices.

There is no scientific way to determine how large one's conventional forces should be. It is not possible to determine whether the forces of one side or the other are in some static sense superior, nor can one predict the outcome of a military battle. **In determining** whether forces are of an appropriate size, one needs also to consider alternative ways for a society to spend resources, a potential enemy's responses to an increased effort, the likely warning time of an attack, the potential for reduction of conventional forces through verifiable arms control agreements, and so on. The outcomes of these considerations lead to huge variations in estimates of NATO's conventional requirements.

Having said all of that, it is important to note that the recommended change in posture will, with no increase in spending, produce a very significant increase in the capability of NATO military forces to engage in sustained conventional combat. It would free those resources now devoted to protecting the nuclear storage sites and preparing to deliver nuclear weapons. The funds that go into developing and producing new nuclear devices could be used to improve conventional capability.

THE NEW POSTURE IN A MILITARY CRISIS

If the nuclear posture I propose here were adopted, perhaps the most important change would be in attitude. As Michael Howard has pointed out, the current NATO strategy destroys the morale of the forces and makes it very difficult for them to prepare seriously for war.[13]

Knowing that it is not possible to fight a nuclear war, the NATO military forces essentially look upon themselves as a trip-wire or a plate glass. Their mission is to sustain conventional combat just along enough to make credible the threat to employ nuclear weapons or to negotiate an end to the conflict. They are not expected to have the capacity for sustained conventional conflict, and they do not know how to develop the capability to fight a sustained nuclear war.

The proposed posture would fundamentally alter this situation. NATO commanders would be asked to do something that they know how to do: equip, train, and deploy their forces for sustained conventional operations. Their task would be a familiar one: to hold the enemy as far forward as possible and await the arrival of reinforcements that would permit offensive operations. Told to ignore the existence of nuclear explosive devices, NATO commanders would be free to draw on their military experience and expertise to develop strategies for utilizing NATO's inherent advantages.

As a crisis developed, NATO would instantly have available alert forces with a conventional capability. Military forces could be brought to a fuller state of alert without fear of appearing to threaten the use of nuclear devices and without actually dispersing those warheads. Under the current posture, a great deal of effort and attention would go into deciding whether to disperse the nuclear devices and, if so, to moving them from their storage bunkers. Under the proposed alternative, this effort and attention could be devoted to preparing for or pursuing conventional operations. Military commanders would not be tempted to hold forces in reserve for the expected switch to tactical nuclear operations.

The use of conventional force could be more credibly threatened if NATO adopted the proposed posture. Because it would be easier for the Alliance to make the decision to use force, it could more effectively deter acts other than large-scale overt Soviet military aggression. Discussions of NATO strategy generally proceed as if the only problem were to deter an all-out Soviet invasion across the central front into Germany. But other contingencies might arise, including a Soviet decision to close access to Berlin, the use of Soviet military force to suppress an uprising in East Germany, or a Soviet move into a neutral nation in the center of Europe.

Some observers of the European theater argue that developing a capability for sustained conventional war is irrelevant because the Soviets intend to use nuclear weapons at the outset of any war in Europe. The first thing to be said about this argument is that there is no way to be sure. The Soviet military and political leadership sends a variety of different and conflicting signals. In the years after World War II, the Soviets seemed to be planning primarily if not entirely for conventional military operations. Beginning in the mid-1950s, they developed a capability for tactical military operations; many years afterward, they began deploying nuclear weapons in Eastern Europe. At that point, Soviet doctrine apparently shifted to assume that any war in Europe would inevitably be nuclear, and hence the Soviet Union should seek to strike the first nuclear blow.

Since 1982 the Soviet leadership has pledged that their nation would not initiate the use of nuclear weapons, and Soviet doctrine and force deployments have turned again to emphasizing the possibility of sustained conventional conflict in Europe. Today the weight of the expert opinion on the Soviet military is that first use by the Soviets is far from certain.[14]

Even if the Soviets did initiate the use of nuclear devices, it is by no means clear that the current NATO nuclear posture would be preferable to that proposed here. The current posture was not designed to deal with a Soviet tactical nuclear capability; its basic structure was determined in the early 1950s, when the Soviets had no such capability. Changes since then have been more responses to new technologies and to the vagaries of NATO politics than attempts to match or counter a specific Soviet tactical nuclear capability. As now postured, NATO's nuclear forces are less a deterrent or a counter to a Soviet first strike than a target for such a blow.

Indeed, some who seek to develop a capability to fight a limited nuclear war in Europe have advocated a force posture similar to the one suggested here. If the Soviets fired nuclear devices at NATO troops, it is certainly not obvious that a response using nuclear devices deployed with forces in the field would be effective. NATO's targets, whatever they might be, could be hit more effectively with a separate, invulnerable force directly under the control of the SACEUR. Placing the nuclear forces under central control would also increase the likelihood that an agreement to halt the conflict or an order to cease firing the nuclear explosive devices would be honored. In short, central control would also make possible negotiations aimed at ending the fighting.

In order to deal with unexpected contingencies, the separate NATO nuclear command should have plans to fire on a variety of targets, including Warsaw Pact forces conducting military operations in Europe. It should be remembered at all times, however, that the sole purpose of firing nuclear explosive devices is to signal determination and will, not to fight a tactical nuclear war.

Finally, this approach would permit the United States to adopt a posture in its public statements and arms control negotiations aimed at stigmatizing nuclear explosive devices. The most serious objection now offered to such steps is that they would undermine the credibility of NATO's reliance on nuclear weapons to deter Soviet conventional aggression.

WINNING APPROVAL OF THE NEW POSTURE IN EUROPE

For the past twenty-five years, the United States has urged its NATO allies to improve the conventional war-fighting capability of the Alliance. American leaders have argued that it is important to reduce the Alliance's reliance on nuclear devices. Yet Germany and the other European members of NATO have done remarkably little in response to this pressure from Washington. Their failure to respond can be explained in part by political and bureaucratic inertia. But it is also caused by the nature of the tradeoff that the United States has suggested to the Europeans.

Telling American allies that they should increase their conventional capability so that the United States can reduce its reliance on nuclear weapons is like telling young children that if they eat their vegetables they will *not* be given any dessert. Allies in Europe do not want to reduce reliance on nuclear devices. They still believe what the United States told them in the 1950s: Conventional defense is impossible, so the way to deter war is to plan to use nuclear weapons as soon as war begins. It should not be surprising that contemporary lectures about the need to increase conventional forces so as to permit reduced reliance on nuclear explosive devices have been and will continue to be unavailing.

Again, the role of West Germany is central to this discussion. The great fear of the Germans is that the United States will withdraw from Europe, leaving them alone to face overwhelming Soviet conventional and nuclear power. They believe that any significant increase in European conventional power will lead to a withdrawal of American forces, a reduced reliance on nuclear weapons, or both. At the same time, they worry that if they simply ignore American pressure to improve their military capability, the U.S. Congress might force a withdrawal of American forces from Europe.

Thus, from the original agreement in 1948 of West Germany and other European countries to accept the need for German armed forces to the agreement in 1978 to increase defense spending by 3 percent, the Europeans have always told the United States they will do whatever is necessary to prevent an American withdrawal. They have then done as little of what they promised to do as possible.

It is time to start over and seek to build consensus for a new posture and strategy for the defense of Europe. The place to begin is with the issue of the six American army divisions stationed in Europe and the substantial American air and naval forces in the European theater. These forces were originally sent to Europe as an interim measure until European nations recovered from World War II and were able to defend themselves. Since that time, there have been periodic debates in the United States, particularly in Congress, about whether the troops should be brought home. Because the Europeans have declined to build up their forces or buy the ammunition necessary for a conventional defense, many view American forces as simply a trip-wire to nuclear war. Some members of Congress have argued that the force is larger than is necessary; others have suggested that the plate glass American forces in Germany might force the United States into a nuclear war that it did not want to fight. Many Americans view a large U.S. military presence in Europe as an anomaly.

Yet it is not. Given the need to develop a sensible nuclear policy and still guarantee the security of Europe, it is a fair trade to substitute the permanent presence of a large American military force ready to fight for a nuclear doomsday machine linked to a roulette wheel. It would still leave no doubt in the minds of Kremlin leaders that any war in Europe would entail fighting American forces. As long as events in Western Europe do not pose an acute threat to Soviet interests, the Russians are unlikely to start a war that they know will involve the United States. Even if Soviet military planners were reasonably confident of early success in battle—and NATO can deny them such confidence—the Kremlin well understands the historic determination of the American people to fight on despite defeats until the enemy is forced to surrender, when regions of historic or cultural importance to a majority of its citizens are at stake.

Thus, the first debate about altering NATO strategy and deployments must occur in the United States. If America is to have any hope of moving the Europeans to accept the posture suggested here, it must first come to grips with the need to commit itself to stationing substantial numbers of its forces in Europe for the indefinite future. It must accept that Europe will not be able to defend itself against the Soviet

Union; the "United States of Europe" that Americans hoped would come into existence has not appeared.

Europe remains a collection of sovereign states, each ultimately responsible for its own security. Since Germany is the nation on the front line and the one with the historic conflict with Russia, the question is not whether Europe can defend itself without American participation. The question is whether Germany can defend itself alone.

In the long run the Germans, if they come to feel deserted, could develop the conventional military forces and the nuclear weapons that would enable them to deter Soviet military moves against them. However, nothing would threaten the peace and security of the world more than a German decision to develop such an independent military capability. The Soviets are likely to do whatever is required to prevent this from happening, including invading West Germany. The United States would be forced to respond, and the result would be a nuclear confrontation of the most serious kind.

American policy in Europe must be aimed at preserving democracy in Germany and strengthening the consensus in that nation that it does not need an independent military capability. The key to that objective is for the United States to commit itself to the permanent stationing of large American military forces in Europe. By making this commitment—firmly, solidly, and without seeking quid pro quo—the United States can move Germany and the rest of NATO toward accepting a defense of Europe that is less reliant on nuclear threats.

Consensus on this issue must be embodied in a congressional resolution committing American policy to a military presence in Europe as long as Europeans support that presence. With that commitment in place, the United States can begin to discuss with the Germans and other Europeans the value of restructuring the NATO nuclear posture and improving their capability for sustained conventional combat.

6 COMMITMENTS OUTSIDE OF EUROPE

Most discussions of the possible first use of nuclear devices proceed as if the United States would contemplate such a move only if it were losing a large war in Europe. When American policymakers are willing to discuss the question at all, they generally suggest that the United States would consider using nuclear devices first *only* in the face of massive Soviet aggression in Europe.

When pressed, American officials try to argue that the circumstances under which first use would be considered have narrowed considerably since the 1950s. For example, at a congressional hearing in 1976, Fred Ikle, then the director of the Arms Control and Disarmament Agency, contrasted the public statements of President Eisenhower in 1954 (who noted that nuclear devices had "achieved conventional status in the arsenals of our armed forces") and President Nixon seventeen years later (when he called the use of tactical nuclear weapons "rather ridiculous.") Unlike the 1950s position, Ikle concluded, the United States now would contemplate first use only in the "most extreme circumstances where large scale military aggression threatened the vital interests of the United States and its allies." The implication was that this meant Europe only, not anywhere else in the world.[1]

Ikle's comments hold some truth—but only some. It is true that U.S. policy has moved away from treating nuclear devices as "regular" weapons. It is also true that America's reluctance to use nuclear devices in wars fought outside of Europe in the past forty years has probably reduced the risk that they will be used in future conflicts. It is *not* true, however, that the United States now contemplates the first use of nuclear weapons only in Europe.

In fact, American nuclear deployments throughout the world, as well as U.S. doctrine and war plans, contemplate the use of nuclear devices in a variety of settings. Most of the international crises during which the United States has considered the use of nuclear weapons—from Iran in 1947 to the Persian Gulf in 1981—arose outside of Europe and often in nations that did not possess nuclear weapons. Only in the various Berlin crises has the United States contemplated the use of nuclear devices in Europe.

The danger that the United States might initiate nuclear war—intentionally or unintentionally—may be greatest with American forces outside of Europe because military conflict is much more likely to erupt outside of Europe. However, the diplomatic and military costs of altering this posture are much less severe than they are in Europe. For that reason I advocate a much more radical change in posture.

CURRENT NUCLEAR POSTURE

The American nuclear posture worldwide is not very different from the European posture described in the previous chapter. There is no distinction in the military services between weapons systems or force postures for Europe and those for the rest of the world. The weapons systems deployed by the United States throughout the world are designed, procured, and equipped to deliver nuclear devices as well as conventional weapons. War plans and deployments assume that, if necessary, the president will grant authority to use nuclear weapons.

The extensive nature of the nuclear posture can be best described by considering deployments in several areas and by several military services. As these descriptions will show, every element of what is often considered conventional military power is, in fact, part of the nuclear forces of the United States. The elements that I will describe are deployments aimed at Northeast Asia and the Persian Gulf, which are the two areas where the United States most seriously contemplates using nuclear devices at this time; the nuclear configuration of American ships at sea; and the nuclear capability of the marine and army intervention forces, along with the tactical aircraft that would be deployed with them.

The worldwide American deployment of nuclear weapons is well documented by the authors of two volumes: *Nuclear Battlefields* and the *Nuclear Weapons Databook*. These volumes provide the primary source of information about the characteristics of the American nuclear arsenal.[2]

Northeast Asia

Outside of Europe, South Korea is the only country in the world where the United States admits that it stores nuclear warheads. Government officials will not discuss how many weapons are there or precisely where they are stored. Much can be learned, however, by closely examining public sources, as William Arkin and Richard Fieldhouse did for *Nuclear Battlefields*. According to these authors, some 150 nuclear devices are stored in Korea, including bombs, artillery shells, and atomic demolition devices.

In the past, some of these weapons were stored with American forces stationed very close to the armistice line of the thirty-eighth parallel. Now all of the weapons are reportedly stored at the Kusan air base with plans to disperse them to the American forces stationed in Korea when authorized. Aircraft stationed at this base are on nuclear alert, ready to deliver nuclear devices at a moment's notice. As I will describe below, there are many other U.S. nuclear weapons in the

Pacific mated with delivery systems that could reach North Korea.

The situation in Korea is the closest parallel to that in Europe. The longstanding American threat to initiate the use of nuclear devices if necessary to stop a North Korean invasion is still in effect. There is an American commander on the ground with nuclear forces under his command. He has been told that he would be granted authority to use nuclear weapons if necessary. His forces train both for conventional operations and for the use of nuclear weapons.

The warheads are in a single site well known to the other side and vulnerable to a conventional attack. They might be distributed to forces that were threatened with attack, thus creating a use-them-or-lose-them situation. Even the air base at which the weapons are stored could be in danger of being overrun in a successful North Korean attack.

There is substantial uncertainty about the nature of the conventional balance on the Korean peninsula. As in Europe, the American military is pessimistic about the chances for victory in a conventional war and believes that it will have to use nuclear devices.

The main American nuclear storage site in the Pacific is on the island of Guam, where a variety of nuclear devices are kept for dispersal to forces stationed in the Far East. Among the weapons stored there are nuclear artillery shells and atomic munition demolitions, or ADMs.

In addition, the Pacific fleet is heavily armed with nuclear devices. This large force, which includes six aircraft carriers, is estimated to have some 700 warheads, including 300 for naval warfare and 400 for long-range bombing.

The Persian Gulf

The United States has no forces permanently deployed on the ground in the Persian Gulf area. Thus, if America sought to bring military force to bear on this region, it would have to do so from the fleet that is now deployed in the Indian

Ocean or by bringing in American forces from Europe or from the United States. The Indian Ocean fleet has some twenty-five ships and more than 100 nuclear warheads, including bombs. The army and marine forces that would be moved into the area are also armed with nuclear devices.

The American nuclear threat in this area arises from the fear that the Soviet Union would move into the Persian Gulf to seize the oil fields, which hold a substantial portion of the world's oil reserves. Because the Soviet Union is located closer to the area, it is believed to have a significant conventional advantage. Some argue that the only way to overcome this advantage is to use nuclear devices, which would either be dropped on the passes into the area or used against the Soviet Union itself to persuade the Kremlin to withdraw.

Nuclear Deployment at Sea

There has been some discussion in the literature of nuclear deterrence about the possible use of nuclear devices in Korea and the Persian Gulf. By contrast, almost nothing has been said about the deployment of nuclear warheads aboard the ships of the U.S. Navy. Except for the submarines carrying ballistic missiles, it is the policy of the United States neither to confirm nor deny the presence of nuclear weapons aboard any ship.

In fact, American ships at sea are routinely equipped with nuclear devices for land attack, anti-air operations, and anti-submarine warfare (ASW). The land-attack weapons now in the arsenal are bombs to be dropped from carrier-based aircraft. These weapons have been augmented by the sea-launched cruise missiles (SLCMs) now being deployed on many navy ships, including the battleships that are being brought back into action. The ASW weapons come in two forms: depth charges deployed from ships and bombs to be dropped from land-based naval aircraft. The ASW capability includes some 1900 warheads stationed at sixteen bases around the world. Navy attack submarines carry nuclear-armed submarine rocket missiles (SUBROC); a similar weapon is aboard 150 surface ships.

The navy also has some 400 land-based ASW patrol aircraft, which carry B-57 nuclear depth bombs and rotate to bases around the world. Carrier-based aircraft can also deliver nuclear depth charges. The anti-air weapons, which are fired from missiles, are designed to protect the fleets from air attack. The Navy deployes both surface-to-air missiles and air-to-air missiles on its carrier-based aircraft.

Writing in 1985, Arkin and Fieldhouse estimated that the nuclear-armed ships of the navy then comprised "all of its 13 large aircraft carriers, all 5 helicopter and Marine Corps carriers, two recommissioned battleships, all 112 cruisers and destroyers, 64 nuclear attack submarines, and 61 of 68 frigates."[3] One-third of these ships are normally at sea at any one time.

The navy preparations assume the service will be called upon to use nuclear devices in support of conventional combat on land or even before a land war has begun. In such a war, the navy would use its nuclear devices to destroy attacking aircraft and land-based targets. The navy does not deploy nuclear weapons for ship-to-ship operations and, hence, would attack other surface ships with conventional weapons. It has no defense against nuclear-tipped missiles, and many critics do not believe that the major fleets centered on aircraft carriers could survive in a two-sided nuclear war at sea.

The carrier-based bombs are designed to attack enemy installations on land. In the 1950s they were part of the general nuclear war plan, and their primary mission was to attack targets in the Soviet Union in the event of global nuclear war. Since then, their primary mission has been to attack designated targets in limited nuclear wars. The nuclear-armed cruise missiles would perform that role as well, while serving as a reserve force for a protracted general nuclear war with the Soviet Union.

Wherever U.S. naval vessels sail, they are ready to use nuclear devices immediately against targets at sea or on land. Naval doctrine states that these ships must be able to engage in conventional combat as well as deliver nuclear warheads.

Nuclear Deployments with the Marine Corps

Anyone not familiar with the full scope of American nuclear force deployment is likely to think of the U.S. Marine Corps as a conventional force ready to intervene around the world in limited, nonnuclear conflicts. Nothing could be further from the truth. The marines, like the rest of the military services, are determined to share in the budgetary resources for nuclear forces and to be ready to participate in nuclear war. Marine plans for combat include the capability to move nuclear devices ashore by helicopter or landing craft for use by marine units engaged in an amphibious landing operation. In *Nuclear Battlefields*, Arkin and Fieldhouse describe the nuclear capability of the marine corps as follows:

> The U.S. Marine Corps . . . has about 400 nuclear warheads of seven types. Two types of specialized nuclear units—Nuclear Ordnance Platoons (NOP) for ground weapons and Marine Wing Weapons Units (MMWU) for air-delivered bombs—belong to each of the three active Marine Divisions and Marine Air Wings, respectively. Each NOP has sixty nuclear weapons technicians who are responsible for 155mm and 8-inch nuclear artillery and medium and special atomic demolition munitions. The MWWUs have forty-nine technicians each, who provide technical support to Marine aircraft units that use nuclear bombs.
>
> The Marine Corps' nuclear-capable aircraft include the A-4 and A-6, which have had nuclear roles for over two decades. The F/A-18 fighter/light attack aircraft is beginning to replace the Marines' F-4N, which is not nuclear certified, and "will more than double" the number of nuclear-capable Marine Corps aircraft. . . .
>
> In 1981 the new nuclear-capable M-198 155mm howitzer began to replace non-nuclear 105mm howitzers in all three Marine divisions. . . . The Marines also use Medium and Special Atomic Demolition Munitions (ADMs).[4]

Nuclear Deployments with the Army

Army units in the continental United States and those earmarked for operations in countries outside Europe are also equipped and trained to use nuclear weapons. Nuclear artillery shells and the artillery pieces to fire them belong to all army divisions. In the early 1980s, the army developed specific plans to couple nuclear-equipped Lance missiles with its so-called light divisions for foreign intervention. Army divisions are also equipped with surface-to-air missiles that have nuclear warheads and with atomic demolition munitions for the destruction of topographically significant areas, such as mountain passes. Some of the ADMs are meant to be used by unconventional warfare forces. Tactical planes for support of ground combat operations are also equipped with nuclear devices.

In short, the military services simply do not have any sizable forces committed solely to conventional military operations. All of the so-called general purpose and rapid deployment forces are equipped with nuclear weapons and are ready to use them in combat. All plans for combat operations around the world include an annex for nuclear operations based on the assumption that nuclear devices are weapons that can be used in war and that permission to use them will be granted if necessary.

The existing worldwide nuclear force deployments, like the European posture, were set in motion during the Eisenhower administration and have been altered only slightly since that time. Despite increasing evidence that the United States is unlikely to use nuclear weapons in regional conflicts, its nuclear posture continues to reflect the assumption that any conventional war would become nuclear.

If the United States has managed to avoid using nuclear weapons since 1945 despite the deployment of nuclear forces throughout the world, does the current deployment make any difference? I believe the existing posture has a number of serious costs—not the least of which is that it increases the risk of nuclear war.

ALTERNATIVE NUCLEAR POSTURE

Application of the alternative nuclear posture proposed here to areas outside Europe would begin with the assumption that American military commitments can and should be met with conventional forces. Because nuclear devices are not weapons and cannot be used in military conflict, the United States should never contemplate first use of nuclear devices. If an opponent initiates the use of nuclear weapons outside of Europe, the United States could respond with nuclear devices, if it chose to do so, by deploying nuclear forces from Europe or the United States.

The president should issue a directive telling the military services that they should not request and will not receive permission to employ nuclear devices outside of Europe. The United States should procure and deploy its forces, develop its war plans, and make its commitments to defend allies on the assumption that nuclear devices do not exist.

Guidelines for developing new weapons systems should require that they be designed to deliver conventional weapons. War plans should assume that nuclear devices will not be used. In evaluating existing and future commitments, the United States should consider only conventional operations. In a crisis, any decision to employ American forces should be based on the assumption that nuclear devices will not be used, no matter how badly the war may be going.

The military forces stationed abroad, except for the special nuclear command in Europe, should not have nuclear devices with them nor any plans to receive them. All American naval ships at sea (except for ballistic missile-firing submarines and any ships that are part of the NATO nuclear command) should not have nuclear devices on board.

Perhaps most important, the United States should show no hesitation in making this no-first-use policy public and assuring other nations that American ships calling at their ports do not have nuclear devices on board.

In the past, the United States has made two limited commitments of no first use. In connection with the nuclear-free zone in Latin America, it promised not to use nuclear weapons first against a nonnuclear power unless that state was engaged in aggression in alliance with a nuclear power. Later, Secretary of State Cyrus Vance generalized this commitment by stating that the United States would not use nuclear weapons against a nonnuclear-weapons state unless it was allied with a nuclear-weapons state in a conflict with the United States or its allies. However, these disclaimers were carefully written to exlude all situations in which the United States would contemplate using nuclear devices.[5]

If the alternative nuclear posture is adopted and applied to non-European forces, the United States should make clear, publicly, that it would never be in the nation's interest to use nuclear devices first outside of Europe.

OBJECTIONS TO THE ALTERNATIVE POSTURE

The major objections relate to the defense of Korea, deterring Soviet military operations in the Persian Gulf, and the implications of removing nuclear devices from navy ships at sea. None, in my view, are substantial enough to stand in the way of adopting this posture.

South Korea

It is difficult to understand why the United States might need to use nuclear devices to defend South Korea. As in Germany, questions of political and conventional military balance play more important roles in deterring an invasion. In view of the uneasy relationship between North Korea and its two Communist neighbors, and the clear commitment of the United States to the defense of South Korea, it is very unlikely that the North Korean government is even contemplating an attack on the south. Moreover, South Korea is larger and substantially richer than North Korea and has larger military forces. It should be able to defend itself against a North Korean attack without any help from American military forces, let alone nuclear weapons.

At the very least, South Korean forces and American forces still stationed in Korea are capable of stopping a North Korean advance within the Korean peninsula so that American reinforcements could be brought in to turn the tide. Even in the extraordinary circumstance that the Russians or the

Chinese chose to intervene and fight in a war confined to the Korean peninsula, the United States could and should bring enough military power to bear to win conventionally.

Obviously, the United States should seek to negotiate an end to the conflict on satisfactory terms. However, if that is not possible, it would always be preferable to increase the American conventional commitment than to use nuclear devices. The introduction of such devices can only lead to the destruction of the peninsula, if not to a wider nuclear war. It cannot lead to a military victory in Korea.

Even if they accept this analysis, some still argue that the threat to use nuclear devices first helps to deter a North Korean attack, and that the presence of nuclear devices helps to make that threat credible. In the case of North Korea, which has no reliable nuclear ally, this threat may have some residual credibility and hence add to deterrence. However, one must ask whether such threats are, in fact, necessary and worth their cost.

From time to time, proposals are made to withdraw American forces from Korea. It would be far better to commit the United States to keeping armed forces in Korea than to threaten the use of nuclear devices. It would even be preferable to move American forces back to the front line or to improve Korean conventional forces. However, none of these steps are necessary. The conventional balance in Korea and the presence of American forces is as credible a deterrent as one is likely to have anywhere in the world.

Initial opposition to the new posture from the Korean government would be strong, but it would not lead to any fundamental changes in Korean policy. The new posture would reduce the risk of nuclear war without inviting a conventional one.

Persian Gulf

There can be no doubt that the Persian Gulf scenario has become the central concern of the nuclear-threat advocates within the national security establishment. Europe is considered a problem, but only because of intra-alliance difficulties; few actually fear a Soviet attack in Europe. By contrast, there is a belief that the nuclear threat plays an important role in deterring Soviet military moves into the Persian Gulf region.

It is difficult to come to grips with this concern since there is no evidence to support the proposition that the Kremlin has considered making a military move into the Persian Gulf and is deterred from doing so only by the American threat to use nuclear devices. Rather, the argument within the national security establishment is simply that, since the Soviets appear to have military dominance in a region with vast oil resources and have not moved, it must be because they are deterred by the threat of nuclear weapons.

As in the case of Europe, there is no reason to believe that the Soviet leadership is prone to use military force to fill any possible political vacuum. As long as there is no threat to Soviet interests developing in the Middle East, and as long as the Russians are seeking to sell oil and gas to the West, they are unlikely to use force to invade a Persian Gulf state. The Kremlin knows that such a move would probably lead to a direct superpower confrontation, which it has done so much to avoid. In any event, explicit nuclear threats need not be part of the deterrent.

There are two other steps that the United States can take to protect its interests in the region. Both are more effective and less dangerous than relying on nuclear threats.

First, America can reduce its reliance on Middle East oil by building up its strategic petroleum reserve and developing alternative sources of energy. Second, it can increase the credibility and the effectiveness of an American threat to intervene militarily with conventional forces. The Pentagon has improved its ability to move forces into the Persian Gulf region, but it has done so in a way that is designed primarily to increase the credibility of the nuclear threat. The United States should instead make clear exactly which Soviet actions would lead to an American military response, and then develop realistic plans for such contingencies. The United States cannot be sure of preventing Soviet incursion into the area, but it can develop military plans to engage in a holding action until it can mobilize the necessary conventional resources to win the conflict. At the same time, the administration would need to educate the American people about the region's importance and the need to use American military power in its defense. Without public support, it is unlikely that either conventional military power or nuclear warheads would be used, and neither threat would be credible.

Such steps would confront the Soviets with the following threat: If they cross the line drawn in the Persian Gulf region, the United States will respond and involve the Soviets in a direct confrontation with American military forces. The Soviets may or may not have a significant advantage in the opening phases of the war, but, in any case, they will be killing American boys. Soviet leaders must assume that in such a situation, the United States would fight on until the Soviets decided to withdraw.

The American leadership would make it clear that if the Soviets used nuclear devices, the United States would respond in kind, but that it would not initiate a nuclear attack. The American military services would be required to make plans for intervention knowing that nuclear devices would not be available, although an increase in conventional military power would be acceptable. Despite the no-first-use statement, the Kremlin would also continue to prepare for the possible use of nuclear weapons by the United States; Soviet planners would not be content to place full confidence in U.S. public promises not to use them first.

I doubt that any serious student of Soviet behavior would argue that the threat outlined above would not be sufficient to deter the Soviets. It would be at least as credible as the current nuclear threat, and it would eliminate the Persian Gulf problem as a barrier to adopting the posture proposed here.

Nuclear Devices Aboard Ship

Finally, there is the question of the consequences of removing nuclear devices from ships at sea. The important question is this: Does the presence of nuclear weapons on board American ships contribute significantly to deterring military actions or to reassuring allies?

Because of the "neither confirm nor deny" policy, the navy does not admit to having nuclear weapons on ships. Thus, the United States could remove the nuclear weapons from all ships at sea and say nothing.

It is difficult to envision a situation in which the United States would want to initiate the use of nuclear weapons at sea. The large American fleets—with huge and vulnerable aircraft carriers—would not be able to survive a concerted Soviet nuclear attack using cruise missiles or other nuclear weapons. To initiate nuclear attacks on Soviet surface vessels or submarines is to invite a response that would lead quickly to the destruction of the fleet.

For that matter, it is nearly as difficult to imagine the Soviets initiating a nuclear exchange at sea. If they did so it would almost certainly be an all-out attack designed to destroy the U.S. fleets in the battle zone. There is no effective defense, nuclear or conventional, against such an attack.

The nuclear warheads aboard American ships might be of some value in defeating an attack on the fleet with conventional weapons if the United States were willing to use them for that purpose, and if such use did not invite a nuclear response. It is doubtful, however, that the United States would do so. U.S. ships have never come under attack in any of the limited wars in the past forty years. Because of America's overwhelming naval superiority today, future opponents are likely to exercise similar restraint. Even if a sudden attack were to occur, the United States would not want the captain of a ship to react with nuclear devices without authority from the president, and such authorization would not arrive in time to save the ship.

Simply stated, American fleets can better survive and contribute to military objectives in a nonnuclear environment. Moreover, the United States should not break the moratorium on using nuclear devices to defend ships that would be destroyed by a nuclear response.

IMPLEMENTING THE ALTERNATIVE
POSTURE THROUGHOUT THE WORLD

The posture proposed here would significantly reduce the risk of nuclear war in a number of ways. First, by removing the nuclear weapons now deployed at forward bases and on ships at sea, it would remove the risk that nuclear devices would be used without authorization in the heat of combat. Second, it would also eliminate the use-them-or-lose-them danger, since no troops now on the line or sent into combat would have nuclear weapons with them. And third, it would permit the United States to move its conventional forces to a higher alert status worldwide without dispersing nuclear devices or increasing the risk of their accidental or unintended use.

Along with the European posture proposed in the previous chapter, the adoption of the worldwide posture proposed here would permit the United States to move toward stigmatizing the use of nuclear weapons and to emphasize their lack of utility in military combat. The United States could support and even vigorously push for measures such as nuclear-free zones. Coupled with the proposals for strategic forces described earlier, this posture would permit support for a test ban treaty and for a cutoff in the production of fissionable material.

U.S. support for these arms control measures, combined with a public no-first-use policy, should make a significant contribution to preventing the spread of nuclear weapons. Nonnuclear states have been quick to point to the contradiction between American efforts to persuade them to forgo independent nuclear forces and U.S. insistence on its right to initiate the use of its nuclear weapons "whenever necessary."

This posture would also help to avoid situations in which the president was under pressure to use nuclear weapons to meet a perceived commitment to any ally or to the American military. All interested parties would be on notice that the United States would meet its military commitments without resorting to the use of nuclear weapons.

Adopting a policy of not storing nuclear weapons abroad or on ships would, of course, enable the United States to abandon its policy of neither confirming nor denying the presence of nuclear weapons at bases or aboard ships. This would remove a major irritant in relations with many allies, including New Zealand, which in 1985 banned U.S. ship visits because it could not get assurances that nuclear weapons were not on board. It would also eliminate the ever-present danger of a crisis in U.S.-Japanese relations, which could occur if an accident or some other event made it impossible to deny that there were American nuclear devices aboard ships in Japanese ports.

The capacity of the military services to fight conventional wars would be significantly increased. Alert forces would be ready to deliver conventional munitions and could do so much more quickly in a sudden crisis. Training and planning would focus on conventional war. As in Europe, the morale of the forces would improve since they would be planning for wars that could be fought and won rather than for conflicts intended to serve as holding tactics until the battlefield was destroyed with nuclear devices.

In some sense, adoption of this policy would simply conform the official U.S. doctrine on use of nuclear devices to reality. Over the past forty years, American presidents have demonstrated great reluctance to authorize the use of these devices. They have recognized that nuclear devices are not weapons whose use can, even in wartime, be left to the military. They have understood that the use of nuclear devices could not be justified to win a battle and that any use would run the risk of destroying the world.

Thus, the United States has had a de facto no-first-use policy. Yet the military services have been directed to plan as if nuclear weapons *would* be available, and they have continued to possess authority to deploy the warheads and to purchase weapons systems for their delivery. This pardox has contributed to a sense of unreality in all military planning, reduced America's capacity to fight, and increased the risk of unintended nuclear war.

The costs and difficulties of adopting this posture would not be nearly as great as those of adopting the changes proposed for Europe, even though these changes are more far-reaching. The administration would, of course, want to discuss the proposed changes with America's allies—both those directly affected and allies in Europe—before they were put into effect. Any doubts and concerns of the Korean government could be assuaged by committing the United States to maintain a significant military presence in Korea until the situation there was fundamentally altered. This would be a price well worth paying for dismantling some of the most dangerous portions of the doomsday machine. Few, if any, governments elsewhere would object to these changes, and those that do would have great difficulty pressing their objections, given the strong antinuclear sentiment in most countries of the world.

7 ARMS CONTROL

From the time the American people first learned of the Manhattan project more than forty years ago, U.S. efforts at promoting international arms control have been undermined by a tense dichotomy between public and secret calculations—between the desire to rid the world of nuclear weapons and the perception that a credible nuclear threat is necessary to protect the security of the United States.

This dichotomy has influenced every presidential administration and every arms control proposal in the nuclear age. The Truman administration was confronted with it soon after World War II, when the United States presented the Acheson-Lilienthal (Baruch) plan for the abolition of nuclear weapons. In public, the United States eagerly sought an agreement that would permit it to destroy its small stockpile of nuclear devices and to prevent others from manufacturing such devices. Privately, the national security establishment feared that the Soviet Union, not yet a nuclear power, would accept the proposal, forcing the United States to find a way to avoid an agreement.

This dichotomy has persisted right up through the presidency of Ronald Reagan. The "Star Wars" plan he unveiled in 1983 would set up a series of orbiting satellites designed to destroy incoming ballistic missiles. In public, Reagan said that if the Star Wars technology were successful, the United States should be willing to share the necessary technology, allowing the Soviets to protect themselves from American missiles as well and leading to an international agreement making nuclear weapons "obsolete." Privately, however, the national security establishment was concerned that an international Star Wars agreement—and Soviet possession of the Star Wars technology—could undermine the American commitment to Europe and encourage a "fortress America" mindset in the United States.

The conflict came clearly into public focus after the Iceland summit of 1986. The national security bureaucracy reacted with great concern to the possibility that the president would agree to eliminate all ballistic missiles or even all nuclear weapons. Implementing these proposals would nulify the American policy of relying on threats of first use.

HISTORY OF THE ARMS CONTROL DICHOTOMY

Throughout the history of the nuclear age, the American arms control dichotomy has consistently undermined efforts to achieve international arms control agreements.

The most dramatic and long-standing example here is the nuclear testing issue. Beginning in the mid-1950s, as the pressure to end atmospheric testing grew, the United States found it necessary to commit itself to seeking a nuclear test ban treaty. At this time, American policy reflected the "regular weapons" model—that is, the military services were planning on the assumption that nuclear weapons would be used in any conflict. Inside the government and outside, many argued that the United States should not support any activity whose aim was to stigmatize nuclear weapons; nor could it affort to halt the testing necessary to develop the warheads for the delivery systems, including ICBMs, just coming off the production lines.

The approach was the usual one for that period. Publicly the United States would support a nuclear test ban treaty. Privately it would make sure that one would not be negotiated. When the pressure for an agreement became too great, a compromise emerged: the "three-environment" treaty, prohibiting tests above ground, under water, and in space. The treaty still permitted testing underground, and the Joint Chiefs were promised a vigorous continuing test program.

From that time until the mid-1980s, the United States was publicly committed to a comprehensive test ban treaty, but within the government it was understood that such a treaty was unacceptable. This understanding arose largely out of the view that nuclear devices were weapons to be used in combat. If the military was planning to use the devices in combat, then the United States needed to be able to test them. Moreover, it needed to develop new warheads for the delivery systems coming off the production lines. On-site inspection as a means of verification was used as the "joker" to ensure that no agreement was reached.

A serious effort to negotiate a comprehensive test ban may have been undertaken during the Carter administration. The Reagan administration has been explicit about its posture by refusing to resume the negotiations on a complete test ban and stating that such an agreement would not be acceptable on security grounds until there was total nuclear disarmament, even if the inspection issue could be resolved.[1]

Beginning in 1958 with the preparations for a conference with the Soviet Union on how to reduce the danger of surprise attack, a new element was added to the arms control equation. Some members of the national security bureaucracy began to recognize that international agreements might in fact be desirable and negotiable. These officials came to see that some objectives of national security could in fact be enhanced by international agreements, if those agreements could be used to constrain the forces of both sides so as to avoid situations in which war might occur by accident or miscalculation.

This new approach took hold in the government in 1968 with the commitment to begin negotiations with the Soviet

Union actually intended to reach an agreement on limiting the strategic forces of the two nations. There were a number of clear signs that these negotiations were viewed differently by the national security bureaucracy. The existence and capability of American reconnaissance satellites for the first time made it possible to negotiate agreements that would be adequately verified by what came to be called "national technical means." The first sign that this was a real effort to reach agreement was the U.S. willingness to put forward proposals that did not require on-site inspection. The intelligence community was brought into the process and asked to certify its ability to monitor Soviet compliance, within certain limitations.

A second sign of seriousness was the manner in which the proposals were evaluated. The Joint Chiefs of Staff assigned the task to a new unit staffed by officers with analytical skills and headed by a general who understood that arms control agreements could enhance national security.

To signal this new posture the United States approached the Soviets in secret and suggested that the negotiations be conducted in secret. The Kremlin accepted, beginning what became known as the Strategic Arms Limitations Talks, or SALT.

But the initiation of real negotiations only served to highlight the contradiction in American policy. The ostensible objective of SALT was to reduce the risk of nuclear war. This was to be done by measures that "stabilized" the nuclear balance and supposedly reduced the incentive for either side to strike first. Though the Anti-Ballistic Missile treaty did, in fact, make it harder to threaten the use of nuclear weapons credibly, the numerical limits agreed upon in SALT had little effect on either the risk of nuclear war or the credibility of the nuclear threat. There was no way to reduce the advantage of striking first without also reducing the credibility of the American threat to strike first in the event of successful Soviet conventional or theater nuclear attacks. It is not an accident that the United States insisted in SALT II on the right to deploy a new multiple-warhead (MIRV) missile, or that the MX, which is a large MIRVed missile now being deployed, is designed to attack hard targets in the Soviet Union, including missile silos.

As long as the United States adheres to the special weapons model and views nuclear devices as battlefield weapons whose use it would initiate if necessary, the contradictions in American policy will prevent serious additional progress in arms control talks. Moreover, any agreements on offensive forces would not get to the heart of the problem. Since they would be designed to ensure that the United States retained the capability to strike first, they could not eliminate the spiraling fears of first strike.

THE THIRD MODEL OF
ARMS CONTROL

In contrast, the adoption of the third model I described in Chapter 3 would also permit a fundamental change in the American arms control posture. Once the United States accepts as the basis of its policy the proposition that nuclear devices are not weapons for fighting wars, the contradictions that have plagued American arms control policy would be eliminated. It would then be possible to implement fully the insights and verification advances that were incorporated into American policy in the late 1960s. Arms control and the effort to negotiate international agreements would be seen not as an alternative to unilateral policy, not as an entirely different means of assuring American security and survival, but rather as a complement to such policies in pursuit of a single set of objectives.

The United States and its allies would be able to use arms control to implement the view that nuclear devices are not weapons of war or instruments of policy. Their sole objective in negotiations would be to reduce the likelihood that nuclear devices would ever be used—whether deliberately or by accident, whether by the United States, the Soviet Union, or a third power. Arms control would then focus on two sets of negotiations: those aimed at stigmatizing nuclear weapons and preventing their use locally and those aimed at helping to stabilize the strategic nuclear balance.

STIGMATIZING NUCLEAR WEAPONS

The adoption of the third model would permit the United States to focus its efforts on stigmatizing nuclear weapons worldwide without raising concern that such efforts would undercut key components of American security. The United States would not only deny the utility of first use but would stigmatize the second use of nuclear weapons if such use was intended to be effective on a battlefield.

As I have stated previously, under current nuclear doctrine, American efforts to "educate the citizens of allied nations about the realities of the nuclear age" are aimed at persuading them to permit the storage of nuclear weapons on their territory, to permit ships to call at their ports without revealing if there are nuclear warheads aboard, and to rely on the American threat to use nuclear weapons first. Efforts to control nuclear weapons are also evaluated in light of the perceived need to continually modernize the nuclear stockpile and test new and existing nuclear warheads.

The adoption of the approach I have suggested would, in one stroke, eliminate all of these constraints. The United States would not be seeking permission to store nuclear warheads on allied territory nor to have ships with nuclear weapons on board call at ports. It would not need to convince its allies that nuclear first use is a credible threat. The military would be free of the responsibility to develop and test nuclear devices as battlefield weapons.

Thus, the objectives of American arms control policy would be free of ambiguity. The fundamental goal of negotiation and agreement would be to gain support for the new military posture. The United States would support measures reinforcing the view that nuclear devices are not weapons and cannot be used to fight wars. Rather than opposing antinuclear movements around the world and the agreements they promote, it would be supporting such movements and agreements. Though not eliminating the use of nuclear devices as a tool of international diplomacy, the United States would want, as these movements do, to stigmatize these devices and to emphasize the fundamental gap between them and instruments of war.

More specifically, the American objective would be to move all nuclear devices off the front lines and to stimulate the Soviet Union to withdraw its nuclear devices to its homeland. The United States could also take further steps to slow or prevent the proliferation of nuclear devices.

The agreements that would grow out of this approach are familiar ones that have been on the international agenda for many years. The difference is that the United States has, to date, opposed some of them and only pretended to support others. It would now vigorously pursue them all.

First on the list would be the nuclear test ban treaty. If the military services were told to plan as if nuclear devices do not exist, and if the U.S. government proceeded on the assumption that nuclear devices cannot be used to fight wars, then the American objections to a comprehensive test ban treaty would vanish. It would no longer need to fine-tune nuclear weapons for war-fighting roles on the battlefield. The inspection issue would be exposed for the sham that it is. Whatever validity it does have, stemming from the fear that the Soviets could cheat and gain an advantage, would be eliminated by the insight that the devices are not for fighting wars. Small differences in their capability are therefore insignificant.

Negotiation of a comprehensive test ban would reinforce the perception that nuclear devices cannot be used in war. It would also contribute significantly to slowing the spread of nuclear weapons. Many potential nuclear powers have signed the limited test ban and would find it difficult not to sign the comprehensive ban even though they have refused to sign the nonproliferation treaty.

Another agreement long on the international agenda that should be susceptible to negotiation would be a cutoff of the production of fissionable material. If the United States cut back substantially on its arsenal of nuclear devices, it would not need to continue manufacturing fissionable material for nuclear weapons. Moreover, if it no longer thought in traditional terms of fighting a nuclear war with the Soviet Union, it would be much less concerned about possible disparities in the size of the nuclear stockpiles. This would, in turn, reduce concerns about possible cheating on any agreement.

A treaty banning the production of nuclear material would, like the test ban treaty, help to stigmatize nuclear weapons and would thereby contribute to slowing nuclear proliferation. If implemented in conjunction with a nuclear test ban, it would help make clear to the Pentagon and to America's allies that the United States is serious about its new nuclear policy.

The adoption of these policies would also permit the United States to become the major supporter, rather than the chief opponent, of nuclear-free zones and regional agreements not to use nuclear weapons first or against nonnuclear powers. Such agreements, notwithstanding the speed with which nuclear devices could be flown back into combat zones, would reduce the incentives in a crisis to use nuclear devices and would contribute to slowing nuclear proliferation.

The new policy would also enhance America's diplomatic posture. Disputes with nations such as New Zealand about ship visits would be eliminated, as would debates with various governments about nuclear arms control proposals that have strong support within their countries. The U.S. government could use its influence to urge support for its diplomatic initiatives or, where necessary, to press for increases in conventional forces rather than dissipate it in efforts to maintain support for its nuclear policies.

STRATEGIC ARMS CONTROL

In strategic arms control, we can see the implications the new policy would have for establishing international agreements as complements to unilateral actions.

The strategic posture that I have recommended would permit a radical restructuring of the American approach to strategic arms control. Recall that the objective is to develop a capability to ride out a Soviet attack and to respond hours or even days later. U.S. forces would be configured so that they would not be highly vulnerable to an attack and could not destroy a substantial portion of the Soviet capacity to retaliate. The plans for their use would have them move toward survivability rather than swifter use in a crisis.

The United States can and should do much to move in this direction even in the absence of an agreement with the Soviet Union. International agreements should be sought only when the United States cannot accomplish the objective unilaterally or when an agreement can improve the situation.

Obviously, the adoption of this approach would remove the most serious obstacle to American acceptance of strategic arms control agreements, namely, the effort to maintain a credible threat that the United States would strike first. With that objective eliminated, the goal of American strategic arms control policy, like that of its unilateral policy, would be to stabilize the strategic balance by reducing either side's incentive to strike first.

The most important agreement would be one aimed at strengthening the Anti-Ballistic Missile, or ABM, treaty. This is not the place to explore the technical details of how the treaty might be strengthened. Suffice it to say that various issues concerning what can and cannot be tested need to be clarified. The incentives within the Pentagon to renounce the treaty would be greatly reduced because the military would no longer need to concern itself with fighting a strategic nuclear war and because American strategic forces would be protected by other means.

In this context—with the United States stigmatizing nuclear devices as weapons of war—a nuclear freeze would take on new and enhanced meaning. At one level, adoption of a freeze would symbolize the acceptance by both sides of the precept I propose here: Nuclear devices are not weapons with which wars can be fought. Hence the details of the balance are of little importance, and both sides can stop at whatever point they happen to be. They can then begin the process of negotiating reductions and alterations in their force postures to reflect the criteria of the model as outlined above.

Concerns about possible cheating and the details of the freeze would seem much less important once the military understood that it could not fight a war with these devices. American leaders would be less concerned about possible violations, a sudden ending of the agreement, or the precise details of what systems were covered.

Of course, it would be possible to move directly toward a meaningful arms control agreement without the freeze, but a freeze would facilitate agreement on other measures. For one thing, if both sides stopped testing and building strategic forces, it would be much easier to evaluate the implications of particular agreements; they would be imposed on a known and stable environment rather than an unknown and rapidly changing balance. For another, the process of negotiating a freeze could help confirm that both sides accepted the new posture—or at least that the Soviets understood what the United States was up to. Within the American government, support for particular agreements would be greater if it were clear that the race was over and that the United States would not be developing new nuclear systems for fighting wars.

A number of other arms control measures would flow naturally from adoption of the recommended posture. It is difficult to predict, however, whether the Soviets would be interested in them. Much would depend on whether the Soviets were ready to follow the American lead, as occurred in 1968 when the Kremlin accepted American thinking about why defensive systems were "bad." Even if the Soviets did not adopt the U.S. posture, however, they might find some of the agreements of interest.

Briefly, the agreements that would be open to serious discussion would include:

- A limit on the number of warheads on each side at an equal and steadily declining level. With equal numbers on both sides, neither could "afford" to fire more than one warhead at a site that contained only one warhead. Thus, with such an agreement, the United States could make its land-based missile force invulnerable by putting single-warhead missiles into every silo.

- A ban on testing or deployment of new MIRVed missiles and a gradual phasing out of all existing MIRVed missiles. In the absence of ABMs or plans to strike first, multiple warheads are unnecessary. Conversely, phasing out such weapons would reduce the incentive to strike first.

- Agreements to deploy submarines in zones so far away from the other nation's homeland that submarine-based missiles could not reach enemy territory, or, at least, the major strategic nuclear forces of the other side. Ingenuity would be required to develop a way to permit such an agreement to be monitored without rendering the submarines vulnerable to an attack.

- Agreements to permit each side to deploy radars on the other's territory to monitor missile launching more reliably and effectively. Such an agreement, by making a surprise first strike impossible, would dampen preemptive urges in a crisis. Neither side would contemplate going first if it knew that its attack would not be a surprise and if it were confident that it could not be hit by a surprise attack.

- Agreements to permit each side to station observers at the other's missile silos to certify that preparations for a launch were not underway. Such proposals would be especially interesting if each side had built-in delays in its missile firing so that moves toward reducing the time would be visible to the observers. Deep underground silos are one example of such a possibility.

- Agreements not to target the other side's command and control capability. Such an agreement would be difficult to monitor in peacetime but could have some symbolic value.

- Agreements to place nonnuclear explosive devices in missiles, which would permit the missile to be blown up if it were accidentally launched. The current obstacle to such an agreement is that the other side would learn how to disarm American missiles. Such a fear is relevant only if one seeks to strike first. Prior to a retaliatory blow, one could disarm the destruct devices.

For forty years, American arms control efforts have been saddled with a basic contradiction, so that U.S. policymakers have had to engage in subterfuge in order to sabotage arms control treaties in private while, at the same time, American leaders have supported them in public. Applying the third model would free the United States from this web of contradiction and deception. Further, it would allow American leaders to view international agreements as a useful supplement to, but not a replacement for, a less risky nuclear policy at home.

8 CONCLUSION

The 1986 summit conference between President Reagan and Soviet leader Mikhail Gorbachev, and the ensuing public controversy about what had and had not been agreed upon, turned the public spotlight for the first time in many years on the key themes of this book.

As the two leaders sought to outdo each other in their commitment to reducing nuclear arms, they were reported to have agreed on the goal of eliminating all nuclear weapons within ten years. Alternative versions of the proposed agreement indicated that it called only for the elimination of ballistic missiles or of all strategic offensive weapons.

For a time, the White House seemed unable to decide whether it should boast about the president's proposal or deny it. In the end, the president's spokesperson echoed the basic propositions of this book. The American people, he said, urgently wanted the elimination of nuclear weapons and were willing to support proposals to that end, even if it meant some risk to American security and increased spending on conventional forces.

Criticism of the president's reported stand came from the nuclear threat advocates within the national security bureaucracy. They objected not only to the most sweeping proposal but to the more modest versions as well, arguing that they would reduce the credibility of the American threat to strike first with its strategic forces. From the rest of the American public there was support for all three versions and especially for the total elimination of nuclear weapons.

The White House statements seem to suggest that public sentiment on the nuclear question is strong enough even for a Republican administration to consider basic changes in American nuclear policy. Given that fact, the question then becomes how the U.S. government could be persuaded to adopt the policy presented in this book. The fundamental changes in policy suggested here cannot be imposed on the executive branch from the outside. The Congress, even if it were collectively convinced of the wisdom of this approach, would not seek to impose it on the president. The questions then are how to persuade the president and whether a president who wanted to institute such policies could get the necessary support to do so. These questions are, of course, not unrelated. For a president to undertake a sweeping change in national security policy, he must be persuaded both that it is in the national interest and that it can garner the necessary domestic support so that he can successfully implement it without exhausting his political capital.

The first threshold that a president must cross is to believe that the security of the United States does not depend on the ability to make credible threats to use nuclear weapons first. He needs to understand that the conventional balance is not hopelessly or inevitably weighted on the side of the Soviet Union. He also needs to be reassured that America's allies would accept a change in U.S. policy.

The arguments presented in the previous chapters were meant to convince any reader that the adoption of a policy founded on the premise that nuclear devices are not weapons is in fact consistent with U.S. national security interests. There needs to be a public debate both about the proposals presented here and about the dangers of current policy. Future presidents and their advisers must become aware of the particulars of the current policy and of the fact that the United States has a choice.

There are also some specific reasons why any president should be anxious to change the existing policy. Each post-war American president has come to be preoccupied with the danger of nuclear war. Every president has been determined not to use nuclear weapons and has sought to negotiate an end to the nuclear arms race. But few, if any of them, have understood the degree to which the current U.S. nuclear posture increases the risk of nuclear war. They have not understood the degree to which the military expects to get, and plans on the assumption that it will get, permission to use nuclear weapons first. Presidents also have not understood the degree to which Pentagon opposition to arms control proposals proceeds from this assumption and that the assumption flows from presidential directives that have been neither rescinded nor renewed.

Once they understood this, presidents would have every reason to react and to seek a way out of dependence on nuclear weapons. No president wants to be confronted with a demand from the military to use nuclear weapons nor to be told that nuclear weapons went off by mistake.

No one who could be elected president of the United States needs to be told that the American people would accept a policy that involved reduced reliance on nuclear weapons. A president would know that most Americans believe that their government has been working all along for the elimination of nuclear weapons. A president who called for reducing or eliminating reliance on nuclear weapons, and who told the American people that nuclear devices were not weapons and could not be used to fight wars, would find extensive public support for this posture.

Most American presidents have realized this and have sought to change the policy of relying on nuclear deterrence. They have, however, seen only two of the three options that are available. They have looked to technology as a way out of the dilemma and they have sought sweeping agreements with the Soviet Union. But they have not recognized the third option: the way sketched here of redesigning the U.S. military posture so that it can accomplish the same objective, no matter what the Soviets do and without any new technology.

Star Wars and the total elimination of nuclear weapons presume, as clearly as the option I am espousing, that America can defend its interests without nuclear weapons. Negotiating the total elimination of these weapons forces the United States to defend its interests without relying on nuclear weapons by making them disappear from the earth; Star Wars, if deployed on both sides, as President Reagan said he thinks it should be, does so by preventing either side from attacking the other. But neither is practical.

The underlying principle of Star Wars is that neither the United States nor the Soviet Union should be able to threaten to attack the other. Implicit in the Star Wars concept, then, is the abandonment of the basic principle that has guided American policy in the nuclear age: the need to credibly threaten a first strategic strike. If the United States is indeed prepared to give up that threat, then the adoption of the policy presented here has many advantages over the potential rewards of Star Wars.

It can be implemented now without waiting for still-uncertain scientific breakthroughs far into the future. In addition, the effort to develop large-scale defenses on both sides would almost certainly increase the pressure to strike first in a crisis, regardless of the president's benign vision. This is so for two reasons.

First, any strategic defensive system is likely to be vulnerable, or at least appear to be vulnerable, to a carefully planned attack. Thus, the side striking first could begin by destroying the ABM system of the other side. The side receiving the full weight of an attack once its ABM system was suddenly disarmed could not hope to destroy the other side's ABM system in a retaliatory blow.

Second, strategic defenses are likely to work much better when they are in a full state of alert and when they are dealing with a small, ragged attack. Thus, the side striking first could hope simply to overwhelm, if it could not destroy, the defending ABM system, while its defenses handled the smaller but still potentially lethal retaliatory blow.

The proposal outlined here is also preferable to Star Wars for another reason: Star Wars cannot be tested. No one knows how to build a complex system that works perfectly, or even close to perfectly, the first time it is tested. Thus, Star Wars might be able to deflect the fourth or fifth attack designed to destroy it, but it certainly will not successfully ward off the first attack.

Thus, any effort to implement Star Wars without an agreement with the Soviet Union would make the world more dangerous, not less so, and would increase the pressure on a president to authorize a first strike in a crisis. As President Reagan discovered in his summit conference with Gorbachev, any hope of deploying Star Wars by agreement depends on securing a commitment to eliminate all offensive nuclear weapons. Star Wars is then seen simply as a hedge against cheating and the actions of small nuclear powers.

The effort to negotiate the total elimination of nuclear devices, despite its surface appeal, is not an alternative to the posture proposed here. The verification requirements for the total elimination of nuclear weapons are impossible to meet in any real-world context. There would be no way to be certain that the Soviet Union, not to speak of third world countries, had not hidden away nuclear warheads to be taken out in a crisis. Even if all the publicly announced nuclear powers agreed to the most intrusive forms of inspection, weapons might be successfully concealed on their territory or that of a friendly country. Moreover, there would be no way to ensure that other countries, such as Israel or South Africa, did not have nuclear weapons stockpiled. In a world of nuclear disarmament, 200 South African or Israeli weapons would give either of those nations a degree of wholly unacceptable influence.

Moreover, the transition to a nonnuclear world would be almost impossible to negotiate even if all nations agreed on the goal. The phasing out of various nuclear forces and the linkage to verification and to reductions in conventional forces would pose insurmountable problems. An international crisis would, in all probability, derail the agreement long before the final stages were reached.

Perhaps most relevant to this argument, allied and internal American opposition to any such proposal would be strong enough to kill it unless the United States had already adopted the posture I have proposed. The Europeans would object to general nuclear disarmament as giving up even the "existential" deterrence that would remain with the posture presented here. The U.S. military would object as long as it believed it would get permission to use nuclear weapons when "necessary." Thus, the adoption of this proposal is a prerequisite for any sweeping nuclear disarmament. Once the policy was adopted and in place, it might well be possible to negotiate substantial reductions in nuclear forces. However, problems of verification and third party participation would still make complete nuclear disarmament impossible.

Thus a president who wants to get out of the box he now finds himself in should come to see that neither technology nor negotiated agreement is the answer. Rather, the dilemma is largely one that the United States created for itself and that it can resolve to a significant degree on its own. Can a president who reaches this conclusion implement a policy based on the notion that nuclear devices are not weapons and can be used only to deter their use by others? I believe that the answer is clearly yes.

For one thing, the American president has such a commanding position in the U.S. political system that he could make these changes over the strong objections of the Congress and the Joint Chiefs. However, I think that will not be necessary. Congress is always reluctant to challenge the president on a national security issue. It will do so only when public pressure forces it to do so. On this issue the overwhelming weight of public opinion would be on the side of the president.

Consider for a moment a speech by a new president announcing that he had discovered to his dismay that the American military services had built their war plans around the assumption that he would give them permission to use nuclear weapons first and to fire strategic weapons first or a quick second. The president would go on to say that he had immediately taken steps to change this. Without deciding that he would never—even in the most extreme situation—consider using nuclear devices first, he had told the services that these devices were not weapons and they they should plan on the assumption that they would not be used.

The public reaction to such a speech would make congressional opposition virtually impossible. If the Joint Chiefs of Staff objected, some members of Congress would, no doubt, join them. However, they would be drowned out by the chorus of approval from the public and many political leaders.

Moreover, I do not believe that the military services would object strenuously. Asked whether "nuclear weapons" should be available for combat, they will always say yes. But if a president tells them that he will never give them permission to use nuclear devices in combat and that they should plan as if nuclear weapons do not exist, they will accept the decision as coming from a higher level of authority. Many in the military would, I would suggest, heave a sigh of relief. Deep in their hearts most officers do not expect to be granted permission to use nuclear weapons in a local war and they know that much of their planning has an air of unreality.

Many military planners are aware of the high costs of preparing for both nuclear and conventional war. They also know that it is difficult to plan or train seriously for nuclear combat and that it is hard in that environment to sustain morale for conventional combat. At least as many military leaders would openly welcome this plan as would secretly oppose it. The public support for the plan would foil a military effort to undercut it in the Congress.

The key is the public reaction. If the American public favors this policy, the president will adopt it and be able to implement it. If the public does not, then nothing will be done. The answer to reducing the risk of nuclear war is not to hope for a technological breakthrough or a far-reaching agreement with the Soviet Union. Rather, the first step is for the American public to understand that the risk of nuclear war has increased because of decisions made by the government and that those decisions are not immutable. Americans must then devote the energy and effort necessary to change U.S. policy. We must all realize that we have the power to make things better and we *must* use that power.

NOTES

CHAPTER 1: A BRIEF HISTORY OF AMERICAN
NUCLEAR POLICY

1. As far as we know, only one person, Joseph Rotblat, ever tried to stop the program. According to Freeman Dyson, Rotblat was the only scientist to leave the Los Alamos laboratory in December 1944 when it became clear that a German atomic bomb was not a serious possibility. Freeman Dyson, *Weapons and Hope* (New York: Harper and Row, 1984), 131-32.

2. Robert J.C. Butow, *Japan's Decision to Surrender* (Stanford, Calif.: Stanford University Press, 1954).

3. See Gregg Herkin, *The Winning Weapon: The Atomic Bomb in the Cold War, 1945-1950* (New York: Alfred A. Knopf, 1980), 226.

4. David Lilienthal, *The Journals of David E. Lilienthal*, vol. 2, *The Atomic Energy Years, 1945-1950* (New York: Harper and Row, 1964), 391.

5. David Alan Rosenberg, "Reality and Responsibility: Power and Process in the Making of United States Nuclear Strategy, 1945-1968," *Journal of Strategic Studies* 9, no. 1 (March 1986): 38-42.

6. See Lilienthal, *The Journals of David E. Lilienthal*. In April 1950 Truman approved the transfer of a small number of nuclear war-

heads and nonnuclear components to the military. See Richard G. Hewlett and Francis Duncan, *Atomic Shield, A History of the United States Atomic Energy Commission, II* (University Park: Pennsylvania State University Press, 1969), 537–39.

7. David Alan Rosenberg, "The Origins of Overkill: Nuclear Weapons and American Strategy, 1945-1960," *International Security* 7, no. 4 (Spring 1983): 13.

8. See "Draft Report by the National Security Council on United States Policy on Atomic Warfare" (NSC 30), *Foreign Relations of the United States*, 1948, vol. 1, 624–28, and related memoranda by Hickerson, Allen, and Butterworth, 629-31.

9. Rosenberg, "Reality and Responsibility," 38.

10. *Congressional Record*, 81st Cong., 2d sess., March 13, 1950, 96, pt. 3: 3198-3200. For the Flanders resolution, I am indebted to Catherine E. Girrier, "The No-First-Use Issue in American Nuclear Weapons Policy: 1945-1957," draft of master's thesis for the Graduate Institute of International Studies, Geneva, Switzerland, November 1984.

11. The resolution was introduced on June 27, 1949. See "Flanders Asks Use of A-Bomb Only in Case of an Attack," *Washington Post*, 28 June 1949, 7; "Use of Bomb Asked Only to Retaliate," *New York Times* 28 June 1949. See also "Twelve Top Physicists Ask U.S. Not to Be First to Use Hydrogen Bomb," *New York Times* 5 February 1950, 1.

12. George F. Kennan, *Memoirs, 1925-1950* (Boston: Atlantic Monthly Press, 1967), 472.

13. See "Memorandum by the Counselor (Kennan)," *Foreign Relations of the United States*, 1950, vol. 1, 22-44.

14. Senator Mike Gravel edition, *The Pentagon Papers*, vol. 1 (Boston: Beacon Press, 1971), 426.

15. I encountered a number of such references while completing a classified study of the 1958 Taiwan Straits Crisis for the Rand Corporation.

16. Bernard Brodie, *War and Politics* (New York: Macmillan Company, 1973), 61.

17. Gravel, *The Pentagon Papers*, 426.

18. See, for example, Helmut Schmidt, *Defense or Retaliation, A German View*, trans. Edward Thomas (New York: Praeger, 1962).

19. John P. Rose, *The Evolution of U.S. Army Nuclear Doctrine, 1945-1980* (Boulder, Colo.: Westview Press, 1980), 56.

20. Ibid., 73.

21. Aircrew Training Manual for F-100 D/F, PACAFM 51-6, Volume 1, March 1, 1961, cited in Benjamin S. Lambeth, "Pitfalls in Force Planning: Structuring America's Air Arm," *International Security* 10, no. 2 (Fall 1985): 105.

22. John Foster Dulles, "Evolution of Foreign Policy" [Speech delivered to the Council on Foreign Relations, Washington, D.C., 12 January 1954 (Department of State Press Release no. 8)].

23. Matthew B. Ridgway, *Soldier: The Memoirs of Matthew B. Ridgway* (New York: Harper and Row, 1956), 296-97.

24. Maxwell D. Taylor, *The Uncertain Trumpet* (New York: Harper and Row, 1959).

25. This was clear to me while serving as a consultant to the Office of the Secretary of Defense and, after 1966, as deputy assistant secretary of defense.

26. See Public Agenda Foundation, *Voter Options on Nuclear Arms Policy* (New York: Public Agenda Foundation, 1984), 22, for changing American views since 1949 on the use of nuclear weapons.

27. Remarks of Secretary of Defense Robert S. McNamara at commencement exercises, University of Michigan, Ann Arbor, 16 June 1962.

28. Rose, *The Evolution of U.S. Army Nuclear Doctrine*, 124.

CHAPTER 2: THE MYTHOLOGY OF NUCLEAR THREATS

1. See, for example, Public Agenda Foundation, *Voter Options on Nuclear Arms Policy* (New York: Public Agenda Foundation, 1984), 3, 19, 22.

2. Bruce R. Kuniholm, *The Origins of the Cold War in the Near East: Great Power Conflict and Diplomacy in Iran, Turkey, and Greece* (Princeton, N.J.: Princeton University Press, 1980), 304-37.

3. Ibid. See also McGeorge Bundy, "The Unimpressive Record of Atomic Diplomacy," in *Nuclear Crisis Reader*, ed. Gwyn Prins (New York: Vintage Books, 1984), 44-46.

4. It is now clear that no atomic bombs accompanied the B-29s. The United States had a total of only five bombs at that time. Furthermore, the B29s were not even configured to carry atomic bombs. Some argue that the Russians were probably aware that the bombers were not nuclear capable. Gregg Herkin, *The Winning Weapon: The Atomic Bomb in the Cold War, 1945-1950* (New York: Alfred A. Knopf, 1980), 260.

5. Bundy, "The Unimpressive Record of Atomic Diplomacy," 46.
6. Ibid., 49.
7. According to General Maxwell D. Taylor, then chairman of the Joint Chiefs, "it is significant that during the Lebanon landing in 1958, the United States Army had an Honest John rocket afloat off Beirut but was not allowed to land it because it could fire an atomic warhead as well as a conventional one. In this instance, our political leaders felt that it was against the national interest even to suggest by the presence of the weapon that we might use atomic weapons in Lebanon." Maxwell D. Taylor, *The Uncertain Trumpet* (New York: Harper and Row, 1959), 9–10.
8. Bundy, "The Unimpressive Record of Atomic Diplomacy," 49–50.
9. *Public Papers of the Presidents, 1963–4*, vol. 2, 1051, cited in Bundy, "The Unimpressive Record of Atomic Diplomacy," 48. Barry Goldwater had a number of suggestions for making use of atomic weapons in North Vietnam, among them: "I'd drop a low-yield atomic bomb on the Chinese supply lines in North Vietnam" and "Defoliation of the forest by low-yield atomic weapons could well be done." William G. Effros, *Quotations Vietnam: 1945–1970* (New York: Random House, 1970), 206–207.
10. "A Nation Coming into Its Own," *Time*, July 29, 1985, 48–53.
11. Henry Kissinger, *Years of Upheaval* (Boston: Little, Brown, 1982), 583–84; also in Scott D. Sagan, "Nuclear Alerts and Crisis Management," *International Security* 9, no. 4 (Spring 1985): 123.
12. Richard M. Nixon, *RN: The Memoirs of Richard Nixon* (New York: Grosset and Dunlap, 1978), 393–94; also in Sagan, "Nuclear Alerts and Crisis Management," 126.
13. Sagan, "Nuclear Alerts and Crisis Management," 124–25.
14. Jimmy Carter, *Keeping Faith: Memoirs of a President* (Toronto: Bantham Books, 1982), 483.
15. James Reston, "Reagan Is Prepared to Hold Arms Talks If Soviet Is Sincere," *New York Times*, 3 February 1981, 1.

CHAPTER 3: THREE MODELS OF NUCLEAR FORCES

1. McGeorge Bundy, Morton H. Halperin, William W. Kaufmann, George F. Kennan, Robert S. McNamara, Madalene O'Donnell, Leon V. Sigal, Gerard C. Smith, Richard H. Ullman, and Paul C. Warnke, "Back From the Brink," *The Atlantic*, August 1986, 35–41.

2. Thomas C. Schelling, *The Strategy of Conflict* (London: Oxford University Press, 1960), 111.

CHAPTER 4: STRATEGIC NUCLEAR FORCES

1. David Alan Rosenberg, "Reality and Responsibility: Power and Process in the Making of United States Nuclear Strategy, 1945–1968," *Journal of Strategic Studies* 9, no. 1 (March 1986): 35–52.
2. For a fuller discussion, see Morton H. Halperin and David Halperin, "The Key West Key," *Foreign Policy* no. 53 (Winter 1983–84): 114–30.
3. Bruce G. Blair, *Strategic Command and Control: Redefining the Nuclear Threat* (Washington, D.C.: The Brookings Institution, 1985), 282.
4. Ibid., 288.
5. Thomas C. Schelling, *The Strategy of Conflict* (London: Oxford University Press, 1960), 207–29.
6. Richard L. Garwin, "Reducing Dependence on Nuclear Weapons: A Second Nuclear Regime," in *Nuclear Weapons and World Politics: Alternatives for the Future*, 1980s project/Council on Foreign Relations, ed. David C. Gompert (New York: McGraw-Hill, 1977), 83–147.
7. Blair, *Strategic Command and Control*, 289.
8. Ibid., 290.
9. Ibid.
10. Schelling, *The Strategy of Conflict*, 187–203.

CHAPTER 5: NUCLEAR STRATEGY IN EUROPE

1. William M. Arkin and Richard W. Fieldhouse, *Nuclear Battlefields: Global Links in the Arms Race* (Cambridge, Mass.: Ballinger Publishing, 1985), 105.
2. Ibid., 107.
3. Paul Bracken, *The Command and Control of Nuclear Forces* (New Haven: Yale University Press, 1983), 157.
4. Ibid., 167.
5. Ibid., 129–78.
6. North Atlantic Assembly's Special Committee on Nuclear Weapons in Europe, *Second Interim Report on Nuclear Weapons in Europe*, Report to the Committee on Foreign Relations, U.S. Senate, 98th Cong., 1st sess. (Washington, D.C.: Government

Printing Office, 1983), 7. For discussion, see J. Michael Legge, *Theater Nuclear Weapons and the NATO Strategy of Flexible Response*, Rand Report R-2964-FF (Santa Monica, Calif.: Rand Corporation, 1983), 19-20.

7. Kaufmann suggested deployment of some 220 helicopters armed with 880 nuclear missiles. William F. Kaufmann, "Nonnuclear Deterrence," in *Alliance Security: NATO and the No-First-Use Question*, ed. John D. Steinbruner and Leon V. Sigal (Washington, D.C.: The Brookings Institution, 1983), 82.

8. McGeorge Bundy, "To Cap the Volcano," *Foreign Affairs* 48, no. 1 (October 1969): 1-20.

9. Herman Kahn, *On Thermonuclear War* (Princeton, N.J.: Princeton University Press, 1960). ·

10. Thomas C. Schelling, *The Strategy of Conflict* (London: Oxford University Press, 1960), 187-203.

11. For a fuller discussion, see Paul Braken, *The Command and Control of Nuclear Forces* (New Haven: Yale University Press, 1983), 165-72.

12. Ibid., 168-69.

13. Michael Howard, "The Forgotten Dimensions of Strategy," *Foreign Affairs* 57, no. 5 (Summer 1979): 975-86.

14. See, for example, Stephen M. Meyer, "Soviet Theatre Nuclear Forces," *Adelphi Paper* nos. 187 and 188 (Winter 1983-84).

CHAPTER 6: COMMITMENTS OUTSIDE OF EUROPE

1. U.S. Congress, House Committee on International Relations, *First Use of Nuclear Weapons: Preserving Responsible Control: Hearings before the Committee on International Relations*, 94th Cong., 2d sess. (Washington, D.C.: Government Printing Office, 1976), 154.

2. In this section, I draw heavily upon William M. Arkin and Richard W. Fieldhouse, *Nuclear Battlefields: Global Links in the Arms Race* (Cambridge, Mass.: Ballinger Publishing, 1985) and Thomas B. Cochran, William M. Arkin, and Milton M. Hoenig, *Nuclear Weapons Databook*, vol. 1, *U.S. Nuclear Forces and Capabilities* (Cambridge, Mass.: Ballinger Publishing, 1984).

3. Arkin and Fieldhouse, *Nuclear Battlefields*, 62.

4. Ibid., 133-34.

5. Secretary of State Cyrus Vance addressed the United Nations on 12 June 1978. For text, see *Arms Control Reporter*, December 1983, 860-4.2.

CHAPTER 7: ARMS CONTROL

1. According to two Pentagon officials, "Even if verification were not a problem, a CTB would not be compatible with our national defense requirements as long as we depend on a credible nuclear deterrent for our security." "National Security Implications of a Comprehensive Test Ban," text of a presentation to NATO defense officials by Frank Gaffney, deputy assistant secretary for nuclear forces and arms control, and Bob Barker, designee assistant secretary for atomic energy, *Defense Issues* 1, no. 40 (Spring 1986): 1.

BIBLIOGRAPHY

Ambrose, Stephen E. *Eisenhower the President.* Vol. 2. New York: Simon and Schuster, 1984.

Arkin, William A., and Richard W. Fieldhouse. *Nuclear Battlefields: Global Links in the Arms Race.* Cambridge, Mass.: Ballinger Publishing, 1985.

Aspen Institute International Group. *Managing East-West Conflict, A Framework for Sustained Engagement.* New York: Aspen Institute for Humanistic Studies, 1984.

Bahr, Egon. "No First Use." *New York Times,* 10 May 1982.

Ball, Desmond. "U.S. Strategic Forces: How Would They Be Used?" *International Security* 7, no. 3 (Winter 1982/83): 31-45.

Betts, Richard K. "Nuclear Weapons." In *The Making of America's Soviet Policy,* edited by Joseph S. Nye, 97-127. New Haven: Yale University Press, 1984.

_____. "Compound Deterrence vs. No-First Use: What's Wrong Is What's Right." *Orbis* 28, no. 4 (Winter 1985): 697-718.

Blackaby, Frank; Jozef Goldblat; and Sverre Lodgaard, eds. *No First Use.* London: Taylor and Francis, 1984.

Blair, Bruce. *Strategic Command and Control: Redefining the Nuclear Threat.* Washington, D.C.: The Brookings Institution, 1985.

Blechman, Barry M., and Stephen S. Kaplan. *Force Without War.* Washington, D.C.: The Brookings Institution, 1978.

Bracken, Paul. *The Command and Control of Nuclear Forces.* New Haven: Yale University Press, 1983.

Bundy, McGeorge. "No First Use Needs Careful Study." *Bulletin of the Atomic Scientists* 38, no. 6 (June/July 1982): 6–8.

_____. "Early Thoughts on Controlling the Nuclear Arms Race: A Report to the Secretary of State, January 1953." *International Security* 7, no. 2 (Fall 1982).

_____. "The Unimpressive Record of Atomic Diplomacy." In *The Nuclear Crisis Reader*, edited by Gwyn Prins, 42–54. New York: Vintage Books, 1984.

Carver, Michael. "No First Use: A View From Europe." *Bulletin of the Atomic Scientists* 39, no. 3 (March 1983): 22–25.

Charles, Daniel. *Nuclear Planning in NATO: Pitfalls of First Use.* Cambridge, Mass.: Ballinger Publishing, 1987.

Collins, A. S. "Current NATO Strategy: A Recipe for Disaster." In *The Nuclear Crisis Reader*, edited by Gwyn Prins, 29–41. New York: Vintage Books, 1984.

Dean, Jonathan. "Beyond First Use." *Foreign Policy* no. 48 (Fall 1982): 37–53.

"The Debate on No First Use." *Foreign Affairs* 60, no. 5 (Summer 1982): 1171–80.

de Rose, Francois. "Inflexible Response." *Foreign Affairs* 61, no. 1 (Fall 1982): 136–50.

Draper, Theodore. "How Not to Think About Nuclear War." *New York Review of Books*, 15 July 1984, 35–43.

Dyson, Freeman. *Weapons and Hope.* New York: Harper and Row, 1984.

Ellsberg, Daniel. "Call to Mutiny." In *Protest and Survive*, edited by E. P. Thompson and Dan Smith. New York: Monthly Review Press, 1981.

Enthover, A. C. "U.S. Forces in Europe: How Many? Doing What?" *Foreign Affairs* 53, no. 3 (1975): 513–32.

Flaunders, Ralph E. Speech before the U.S. Senate. *Congressional Record.* 81st Cong., 2d sess., March 13, 1950. Vol. 96, pt. 3.

Freedman, Lawrence. *The Evolution of Nuclear Strategy.* London: MacMillan, 1981.

_____. "NATO Myths." *Foreign Policy* no. 45 (Winter 1981–82): 48–68.

Garwin, Richard L. "Reducing Dependence on Nuclear Weapons: A Second Nuclear Regime." In *Nuclear Weapons and World Politics: Alternatives for the Future*, edited by David C. Gompert, Michael Mandelbaum, Richard L. Garwin, and John H. Barton, 83–150. New York: McGraw-Hill, 1977.

Gayler, Noel. "A Commander-in-Chief's Perspective on Nuclear Weapons." In *The Nuclear Crisis Reader*, edited by Gwyn Prins, 15-28. New York: Vintage Books, 1984.

Girrier, Catherine E. "The No-First-Use Issue in American Nuclear Weapons Policy: 1945-1957." Draft of master's thesis, Graduate Institute of International Studies, Geneva, Switzerland, November 1984.

Gompert, David E.; Michael Mandelbaum; Richard L. Garwin, and John H. Barton, eds. *Nuclear Weapons in World Politics: Alternatives for the Future.* New York: McGraw-Hill, 1977.

Gottfried, Kurt; Henry W. Kendall; and John M. Lee. " 'No First Use' of Nuclear Weapons." *Scientific American*, March 1984, 33-41.

Greenwood, Ted. *Making the MIRV: A Study of Defense Decision Making.* Cambridge, Mass.: Ballinger Publishing, 1975.

Herken, Gregg. *The Winning Weapon: The Atomic Bomb in the Cold War.* New York: Vintage Books, 1981.

Howard, Michael. "The Forgotten Dimensions of Strategy." *Foreign Affairs* 57, no. 5 (Summer 1979): 975-86.

_____. "The Issue of No First Use." *Foreign Affairs* 61, no. 1 (Fall 1982): 11-42.

Iklé, Fred Charles. "NATO's 'First Nuclear Use': A Deepening Trap?" *Strategic Review* 8 (Winter 1980): 18-23.

"Is There a Way Out?" *Harpers*, June 1985, 35-47.

Johnson, Stuart S., with Joseph A. Yager. *The Military Equation in Northeast Asia.* Washington, D.C.: The Brookings Institution, 1979.

Kaiser, Karl; Georg Leber; Alois Mertes; and Franz-Josef Schulze. "Nuclear Weapons and the Preservation of Peace: A German Response to No-First-Use." *Foreign Affairs* 60, no. 5 (Summer 1982): 1157-70.

Keenan, George F. *Memoirs 1925-1950.* Boston: Little, Brown, 1967.

King, James E., Jr. "Nuclear Plenty and United War." *Foreign Affairs* 35, no. 2 (January 1957): 238-56.

Kissinger, Henry A. "Strategy and the Atlantic Alliance." *Survival*, September/October 1982, 194-200.

Lambeth, Benjamin S. "Pitfalls in Force Planning." *International Security* 10, no. 2 (Fall 1985): 84-120.

Lee, John Marshall. "The Role of Nuclear Weapons." Mimeo.

Legge, J. Michael. *Theater Nuclear Weapons and the NATO Strategy of Flexible Response.* Rand Report R-2964-FF. Santa Monica, Calif.: Rand Corporation, 1983.

McGwire, Michael. "Dilemmas and Delusions of Deterrence." *World Policy Journal* 1, no. 40 (Summer 1984): 1-12.

Mearsheimer, John J. "Why the Soviets Can't Win Quickly in Central Europe." *International Security* 7, no. 1 (Summer 1982): 3–39.

_____ . "Nuclear Weapons and Deterrence in Europe." *International Security* 9, no. 3 (Winter 1984/85): 19–46.

_____ . "Prospects for Conventional Deterrence in Europe." *Bulletin of the Atomic Scientists* 41, no. 7 (August 1985): 158–62.

Nunn, Sam. *NATO: Can the Alliance Be Sound?* A Report to the Committee on Armed Services. 97th Cong., 2d sess., May 13, 1982. Committee Print.

_____ . "NATO's Nuclear Policy." *New York Times*, 13 May 1982.

Plous, Scott. "No First Use: Having It Both Ways." *Bulletin of the Atomic Scientists* 42, no. 1 (January 1986): 10–11.

Prins, Gwyn, ed. *The Nuclear Crisis Reader.* New York: Vintage Books, 1984.

Public Agenda Foundation. *Voter Options on Nuclear Arms Policy: A Briefing Book for the 1984 Elections.* New York: Public Agenda Foundation, 1984.

Quester, George. "Some Maritime Problems in Avoiding Nuclear War." Mimeo.

Rogers, Bernard W. "The Atlantic Alliance: Prescriptions for a Difficult Decade." *Foreign Affairs* 60, no. 5 (Summer 1982): 1145–56.

Rose, John P. *The Evolution of U.S. Army Nuclear Doctrine 1945–1980.* Boulder, Colo.: Westview Press, 1980.

Rosenberg, David Alan. "The Origins of Overkill; Nuclear Weapons and American Strategy, 1945–1960." *International Security* 7, no. 4 (Spring 1983): 3–71.

_____ . "Reality and Responsibility: Power and Process in the Making of United States Unclear Strategy, 1945–1968." *Journal of Strategic Studies* 9, no. 1 (Summer 1986): 35–52.

Rubin, James. "First Strategic Use: Is It U.S. Policy?" Mimeo.

Sagan, Scott D. "Nuclear Alerts and Crisis Management." *International Security* 9, no. 4 (Spring 1985): 79–139.

Schell, Jonathan. *The Abolition.* New York: Knopf, 1984.

Schelling, Thomas C. *The Strategy of Conflict.* Cambridge, Mass.: Harvard University Press, 1960.

_____ . *Arms and Influence.* New Haven: Yale University Press, 1966.

Schelling, Thomas C., and Morton H. Halperin. *Strategy and Arms Control.* New York: Pergaman, 1985.

Schwartz, David N. *NATO's Nuclear Dilemmas.* Washington, D.C.: The Brookings Institution, 1983.

Shanks, Bob. "The Middle Age of Daniel Ellsberg." *California*, November 1985, 94–96, 118–22.

Sigal, Leon. *Nuclear Forces in Europe*. Washington, D.C.: The Brookings Institution, 1984.

Steinbruner, John D., and Leon V. Sigal. *Alliance Security: NATO and the No-First-Use Question*. Washington, D.C.: The Brookings Institution, 1983.

Treverton, Gregory F. "Managing NATO's Nuclear Dilemma." *International Security* 7, no. 4 (Spring 1983): 93-115.

Tucker, Robert; Klaus Knorr; Richard A. Falk; and Hedley Bull. *Proposal for No First Use of Nuclear Weapons: Pros and Cons*. Princeton, N.J.: Center of International Studies, Princeton University, 1963.

Ullman, Richard H. "No First Use of Nuclear Weapons." *Foreign Affairs* 50, no. 4 (July 1972): 669-83.

_____ . "Denuclearizing International Politics." *Ethics* 95, no. 3 (April 1985): 567-88.

Union of Concerned Scientists. *No First Use*. Cambridge, Mass.: Union of Concerned Scientists, 1983.

U.S. Congress. House. Committee on International Relations. *First Use of Nuclear Weapons: Preserving Responsible Control*. 94th Cong., 2d sess., 1976.

Weiker, Lawrence D. "No First Use: A History." *Bulletin of the Atomic Scientists* 39 (February 1983): 28-34.

Zuckerman, Solly. *Nuclear Illusions and Reality*. New York: Vintage Books, 1983.

INDEX

ABOUT THE AUTHOR

Morton H. Halperin produced this book while on leave from his position as director of the Center for National Security Studies in Washington, D.C. Dr. Halperin served as a deputy assistant secretary of defense in the Johnson administration and on the staff of the National Security Council in 1969. He is the author of numerous books, articles, and monographs on nuclear war and arms control. In 1985 he was awarded a five-year fellowship by the MacArthur Foundation. Over the past several years he has taught or conducted research on nuclear war issues at a number of universities including Columbia, Harvard, M.I.T., and Yale.